Hot Cakes to High Stakes

The Chuckwagon Story

Canadian Cataloguing in Publication Data

Nelson, Doug (Douglas A.), 1950–
Hotcakes to high stakes

Includes bibliographical references and index.
ISBN 1-55059-056-1

1. Wagons—Canada, Western—History.   2.
Wagons—West (U.S.)—History.   3. Chuckwagon
racing—Canada—History. *   I. Title.
TS2025.N44 1993   388.3'41'0971   C93-091299-3

Detselig Enterprises Ltd.
210, 1220 Kensington Road NW
Calgary, Alberta T2N 3P5

Detselig Enterprises Ltd. appreciates the financial assistance for its 1993 publishing program from Canada Council and The Alberta Foundation for the Arts (a beneficiary of the Lottery Fund of the Government of Alberta).

Printed in Hong Kong   SAN 115-0324

This book is dedicated to my father

Lloyd Nelson

Contents

Preface
Acknowledgements

Acknowledgements

My profound thanks to all those people whose words have been used here and all those others who have kindly co-operated with me and have given so freely of their time in the collection of stories to share. My thanks also to those who provided photographs from their family, their company and their organization albums. The Museum of the Highwood, the Glenbow Museum and Archives, the Publication Committee of the Chinook Chapter, and Historical Society of Alberta all gave co-operation above and beyond the call of duty. Those who have read portions of the book at various stages of its development and have given me such helpful comments – you know who you are – I thank you.

Finally, my appreciation to Trudy Cowan, co-ordinator of The Chuckwagon History Project, for her role in editing the manuscript and providing ongoing liaison with the publisher; and particularly for her belief in what this book could be.

Photo credits: *Bob Morrison, front cover and author photo*

Doug Nelson, back cover

Preface

In these days of elaborate working corrals and well-fenced pastures, it is difficult for modern cowboys to comprehend the importance of the chuckwagon to their open range predecessors. Not only did the wagon serve as a mobile camp kitchen, but it was the social, medical and strategic hub of cattle drive and roundup. In many ways the chuckwagon outfit represented an early ranch much more than the shack and corrals from which the wagons trailed every spring and fall.

When, in 1923, cowboy promoter Guy Weadick needed to find a spectacular new western racing event, what better vehicle to represent the old west, what better place to display a cattleman's icon – his brand – than on the cowboys' old "home on the range," the chuckwagon.

Although the chuckwagon's range has been reduced from wheeling across vast grasslands to a race around a half-mile oval track, it still represents traditional western co-operation and community spirit. That spirit is often ignored by popular histories, yet it manifests itself around the chuckwagon barns at racemeets across western Canada, and most particularly in all the assistance I received from the chuckwagon, rodeo and ranching community while producing this book.

generations

It is the first night of chuckwagon racing at the 1991 Calgary Exhibition and Stampede. Sweat-lathered horses, their race completed, prance under harness as their wagons parade in front of the grandstand. They swing around and head back to the barns. The next four competing teams file past them along the outside rail toward the infield.

The second wagon in line is driven by Richard Cosgrave. His father Bob Cosgrave, his grandfather Dick Cosgrave and his great-uncle Dale Flett between them hold 18 Calgary Stampede chuckwagon championships. Two wagons back, at the end of the line is Richard's nephew, Jason Glass. Sitting atop his black-and-white checkerboard wagon, this rookie driver has impressive racing bloodlines as well. Jason is son and grandson of Calgary Stampede champion drivers Tom and Ron Glass and great-grandson of pioneer racer Tom Lauder.

Jason Glass lifts mud-coated outrider's goggles.
(Targhee Photo by Gordon Biblow)

Both Richard and Jason know that the best bloodlines in the world won't help them on the track. The lines that matter there are the four leather ribbons each driver holds in his hands, the lines that string out to his four eager thoroughbreds.

Jason grips those lines firmly as he directs his team toward his barrel position. He concentrates on his horses and barely hears the mellow voice of announcer Joe Carbury declare, "And on barrel number one, driving for Totem Building Supplies No. 2, is 20-year-old Jason Glass from High River. This will be the first run at the Stampede for this fourth-generation chuckwagon driver."

Number one barrel is normally the drivers' choice because it leads directly to the rail – the shortest run around the track. But number one is also a challenge. Its top barrel sits so close to the bucking chutes that there is barely room for the horses and wagon to squeeze through as they execute the top of the figure eight turn.

Jason follows the other three rigs as they head in to make practice turns. As Jason's leaders charge toward the white chute fence he keeps his left lines taut, holding the horses away from the barrel, keeping them from turning until the last moment. Then he pulls his right lines and the leaders fold around the top barrel and complete the figure eight by sweeping left around the bottom barrel. Once onto the racetrack he must quickly haul on his lines to keep his horses away from the Fluor Daniel outfit driven by Wayne Dagg. Jason slows his team and follows the Dagg wagon as it swings around and starts back toward the barrels to start the actual race.

Just ahead of Dagg, Richard Cosgrave turns his head to smile and nod good luck to his nephew. Once the drivers line up at the barrels, family ties are forgotten as each tries his best to be first onto the track and first across the finish line.

Driving toward his starting position, Jason has no time to be nervous. He gives a quick nod to the three

(Targhee Photo by Gordon Biblow)

outriders converging behind him, then lines his horses into position between the barrels. His leader man grabs the lead horses' cross-check lines as the outfit slows and stops. Jason checks to be sure his left hind wheel is not ahead of the barrel. He has barely turned back to his horses when the klaxon blares to start the race.

A shout to the horses! The team lunges forward as announcer Carbury roars, "And theyyy'rrrr offffffffff!!"

(Targhee Photo by Gordon Biblow)

The white bucking chutes loom in front of the charging team. Jason strains to hold them away, but the leaders angle to the right . . . too soon! The young driver's heart sinks as he watches his cramping wagon wheel run over the rubber barrel for a five second penalty.

But the race continues. Jason steers the team safely around the bottom barrel and his horses spurt out onto the racetrack – inches away from Wayne Dagg and Richard Cosgrave.

Into the first turn Jason maintains his advantageous rail position. Hooves cup clumps of moist sand back at him as the outfits round the second turn. Although he is wearing goggles, Jason winces and turns his head to avoid the painful lumps.

Down the backstretch his horses pull alongside the Dagg team and pass them as the two outfits race into the third turn. Cosgrave has eased in behind Dagg to save his horses from running three wide around the last two turns. Tucked behind Jason is the slower turning Wayne Knight rig.

Jason pulls further ahead as he rounds the last turn into the homestretch. He glances back. His white-shirted outriders are all close behind so he slaps his wheelers with the lines and shouts to encourage his horses. First across the finish line, Jason notices the number one barrel still lying on its side. Five seconds of penalty! No time to dwell on his mistake, he completes the parade and hurries his outfit back to the barns.

As soon as he and his helpers have unhooked the horses he runs back across the track to the infield outriders' area behind the bucking chutes. By the time he gets there, his sister

Corry and his grandmother, Iris Glass, have put Jason's outriders' horses into their pen, and are preparing Tom Glass' mounts for the next heat, the last of the evening. Jason runs into the outriders' dressing area, strips off the white driving shirt of his own outfit and dons the yellow outriding shirt he will wear behind his father's wagon. As Jason finishes buttoning his shirt, Iris reminds him that his father also hit a barrel on the first night both years that Tom won the Calgary Stampede.

Jason listens to his grandmother's reassurance. She grew up among the wagons and knows more about the vagaries of chuckwagon racing than anyone on the grounds.

Iris watches another driver, Dallas Dorchester, in the post-seventh heat parade. She knows there are far worse problems than Jason's five-second barrel penalty. For the first time in his twenty-five-year career, Dallas will drive in Calgary without his father, Tom Dorchester, nearby.

"Tom's been so sick this last month that they expect every minute for him to die." Iris says. "Five operations the old boy's had, but he's tougher'n nails; he has that big strong heart and refuses to go – what a long time to wait. Tom didn't deserve all this bad stuff."

"It must be just horrid for the family," she continues, "especially for Dallas. Tom used to be with him all the time. He had his motorhome right in back of Dallas' barn, and was there every day. Probably never told Dallas what to do, but was there with his ideas, to talk to, and to tell those funny stories of his."

With his father Tom in the hospital, Dallas Dorchester's chuckwagon barn was a quiet and sombre place.
(Targhee Photo by Gordon Biblow)

"This year, Tom's not around and Dallas shows it. His mind's not with the wagon. He knows his Dad can't last much longer, so he's hired a bus from his old sponsor Greyhound, to take everybody up to the funeral – when the time comes. I hear Tom was talking about Ronnie [Glass] and Jack [Lauder] in his delirium the other day. With all the rain this spring, when it's rumbling and thundering up in the clouds, I can't help thinking of those two and old Hank [Willard] practicing for the races they'll run soon with Tommy."

Iris has known Tom Dorchester since he started outriding in the 1930s. But her memories of chuckwagons go much further back, back to her grandfather, an ex-North West Mounted Policeman who followed the Cochrane Ranch chuckwagon on roundups, back to her father Tom Lauder, who won the Calgary Stampede chuck-wagon races in 1924, the year Iris was born. She must have been born under a chuckwagon moon.

Genuine smiles all around. Standing, left to right: Joanne Glass, Stampede president Bob Church, Tom Glass and Brent Woolsey. Below, left to right: Tammy Lauder, Norm Cuthbertson, Corry Glass, Jason Glass, Iris Glass and Gary Lauder.

(Bob Morrison photo)

After making their warm-up practice turns, three drivers prepare to swing their outfits back to the infield.
(Targhee Photo by Gordon Biblow)

Before he fires his pistol, the starter must be sure all the wagons and outriders are ready. Note that in 1976 the Ponoka Stampede required only two outriders – one up front to hold the lead horses, the other behind to load the stove.
(Targhee Photo by Gordon Biblow)

At the Calgary Stampede outriders are required behind the chuckwagon – one to load the stove into its rack and two to throw the tent pegs into the back. Stove man Brent Woolsey has his lead shank in his mouth so he can use both hands to lift the bulky, 23 kg (50 lb.) stove. Notice how the stirrup leathers on each saddle are twisted to allow riders' feet to slide in easily after they mount. Notice also how all the stirrups are adjusted short, so riders can stand up and "jockey" their horses.
(Bob Morrison Photo)

When the klaxon sounds the outriders must load the equipment properly before the wagon surges ahead. If they fail the penalties are severe: four seconds for a lost stove, one second for each peg, plus another second if the tarp is dragging or exposed. White chalk lines help drivers, outriders, and judges determine the boundary of each barrel position.
(Bob Morrison Photo)

Most drivers insist that outriders lead their horses past the top barrel before mounting so there is no balky horse in the way when they swing their lead teams toward the bottom barrel. However, some top riders – including Norm Haynes, Frank Dahlgren and Brent Woolsey – consistently jumped their horses at the bottom barrel.
(Targhee Photo by Gordon Biblow)

Quick, agile lead horses and hard-charging wheel horses are essential for a fast, tight rotation around the top barrel. On Calgary's number one position a driver has no choice but to cut it close. There is barely enough room to squeeze an outfit between the chutes and the barrel.
(Targhee Photo by Gordon Biblow)

"Kicking the horses loose" at the bottom barrel is the most thrilling part of a chuckwagon race. This close-up of George Normand captures the intensity of top-flight chuckwagon racing.
(Targhee Photo by Gordon Biblow)

(Bob Morrison photo)

After completing the figure eight turn, outfits on number one and two barrel positions try to protect their favored inside positions while outside outfits attempt to capture, or at least to move closer to, the rail. In this photo the outside driver (Tom Dorchester in the Double AA wagon) is focused on the rail.
(Bob Morrison photo)

A torrid dash to the first bend tests the thoroughbreds' early speed.
(Bob Morrison photo)

Running a wagon's width away from the inside rail for five-eighths of a mile makes a difference of many feet at the finish line. While Edgar Baptiste "goes for it," Richard Cosgrave checks to see if he can edge closer to the rail. (Bob Morrison photo)

On average, outriding horses can travel faster than the chuckwagon horses (they carry only about half the weight pulled by each wagon horse). The safest position for an outrider is near the middle or outside of the track, where there is little chance of interfering or being interfered with. If a rider gets off the barrels slower than the wagon, however, it may be necessary to save ground and take the more dangerous inside route. (Bob Morrison photo)

This race couldn't get much tighter as four wagons thunder down the backstretch! Racetracks with well-designed corners may allow three or four well-matched chuckwagon outfits to travel side by side all the way around the oval.
(Bensmiller Family Collection)

For years Dallas Dorchester and Tom Glass have believed in taking hold of their horses to give them a breather in the backstretch. George Normand used this same technique when he broke the track record at High River in 1992. Here Dallas Dorchester lets his horses resume their charge around the third turn.

(Bob Morrison photo)

In chuckwagon racing, as in other competitive events, some individuals take dangerous and unnecessary risks. Because infractions can happen anywhere on the track, mounted judges watch each section of the race.
(Bob Morrison photo)

At the finish line out-riders must be within 38 metres (125 feet) of the wagon to avoid penalties. Here master tactician Kelly Sutherland slows his leading outfit to give his riders a chance to catch up. (Bob Morrison photo)

Even after completing a full 5/8 mile circuit, Ray Mitsuing's victorious thoroughbreds are not ready to quit.
(Randall A. Wagner)

The past and present come together on the Hooves of History trail drive, Cochrane, 1990.
(Deryk Bodington photo)

origins

Before chuckwagons were ever raced or even seen on the Canadian prairies, the prototype was a hospital unit used by the Union Army surgeons during the latter stages of the American Civil War. A light but sturdy, canvas-covered wagon with an upright chest of medical supplies attached to the back, its hinged end gate protected the chest while travelling, and could be lowered for use as a dispensary or operating table when the wagon reached casualties.

One can imagine a wounded Southern prisoner resting against a tree. As the young Texan awaits his turn under the surgeon's knife, he thinks of home – wishes he was back on the range, rounding up longhorns. A practical lad, he can't help thinking how useful the medical wagon would be if the medicine cabinet were converted to a pantry, its bloody table into a cook's counter. When the war ends and army surplus wagons come up for sale, the young soldier buys one. He scrubs the stains from the table, leaves a few medical supplies in a "possibles" drawer, replacing the rest with coffee, sugar and flour. He replaces the surgeon's instruments with cutlery, hooks up a team of army surplus horses and drives the first chuckwagon home to Texas to surprise his folks.

What started the trail drives was a growing market for beef which could be pastured on wide, open northern prairie grassland. Alberta in the 1890s. (Bradley Collection, Museum of the Highwood)

Studebaker Round-up Wagon.

The above cut represents our ROUND-UP WAGON. It is designed especially for the use of stock men and others wanting a complete camping outfit. It is fitted with a mess box in front of the bed, which has a seat on top, and which is divided into three compartments, lined with zinc and made tight. There is also a large mess box in the hind end of the bed, divided into several compartments, and with three drawers. This is for the purpose of carrying all kinds of provisions and dishes. The box has a lid hinged at the bottom, and this, when let down, forms a table, as shown in the cut.

We use on this wagon our celebrated STEEL SKEINS, and make them in the following sizes : 3 inch and 3¼, both wide and narrow track. The wheels have 1⅝ x ⅝ tire on the front wheels, and 1⅝ x ¾ on the hind wheels, fastened with California rivets. We use long front hounds with wooden top sway-bar ; tight reach ; drop pole, stiffened ; either neckyoke or pole chains, as ordered ; ring on the bottom of the pole to attach lead bars ; foot lever brake, with roller and bar on the top of the hounds, with double draw rod from the roller to the bar ; hind gear, double braced ; bed (wide track, 3 feet 6 inches wide, narrow track, 3 feet 2 inches wide), 11 feet long, 30 inches deep ; foot board and tool box in front ; white canvas top ; bolster springs under bed, if desired, and feed box on each side. Price, $200.00. Coil bolster springs, extra, $8.00 net.

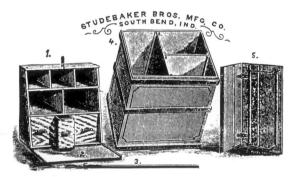

Round-up Wagon Mess Boxes.

The above cut shows the construction and arrangement of the MESS BOXES.

1.—Gives a view of the rear mess box as it appears with the lid dropped to form the table, No. 2 showing the arrangement of the compartments and the three drawers occupying the lower tier.

3.—Shows the standard to place under the table for support when in use.

4.—Shows front mess box tilted forward to give a proper idea of the arrangement of the vertical compartments. The entire box is lined with zinc, and when the cover is down it is perfectly tight.

5.—Shows the hinged cover for the front mess box removed and separate from the box.

These mess boxes are carefully and strongly made, with cleats all around outside, and with the corners fastened with strips of iron.

27

In their 1888 catalogue, Studebaker portrays a well-equipped Round-up Wagon. The Indiana company, however, made no provision for a water barrel – a feature of great importance on the dry prairie.
(Reproduction courtesy Studebaker National Museum)

Innovative cattlemen soon adapted and modified this basic design. As early as 1866, Charles Goodnight and Oliver Loving used custom built chuckwagons on their cattle drives north to the Colorado and Wyoming ranges.

While the Civil War occupied the young men of the American southwest, their longhorn cattle were left to wander and breed and fill the expanse once grazed by the vanishing buffalo. In Texas, these cattle were worth next to nothing, but to the north lay a ready market. With repatriated soldiers chasing them, millions of cattle streamed north to the railheads at Abilene, Wichita and Dodge City. Some of the big ugly beasts, "lanky and cat-hammed," with horns that might measure an impressive and dangerous eight-foot span, were then driven north along the Rockies to help populate the open northern ranges.

Rolling in the vanguard of the trail drive was another western tradition, the chuckwagon. Montana, 1897.
(Glenbow Archives NA-207-104)

The big drives were slow-moving, tedious affairs. Cattle could only travel twelve to fifteen miles a day without losing weight – one huge herd of 25 000 head only moved four to five miles a day. An average sized herd of 3 000 Texas longhorns often took four to five months to reach its Wyoming or Montana destination. The period of these great drives, from 1865 to the 1880s, proved to be the glory years of the American cowboy – celebrated in story, song and in the paintings of artists like Charles Russell and Frederic Remington.

And rolling in the vanguard of the trail drive was another western tradition – the chuckwagon. Because trail bosses avoided populated areas, for months on end the chuckwagon proved to be the hub of the cowboys' social as well as gastronomical life. Many a playing card and many a good story was dealt – and probably worn out – around the chuckwagon's campfire.

At one time, the cook was allotted eleven cents a day to feed each man, so there wasn't much variety in meals. He probably heard a lot of rumbling and grumbling noises erupt from the bedrolls as he went about his last chore of the day, pointing his chuckwagon's pole to the north star, as a compass point for the trail boss in the morning. What with the monotony of the grub, and having to deal with the same human, equine and bovine faces for months on end, it is little wonder the cowboys raised such a ruckus at the end of a long drive.

In December, 1866, the first weary Texas longhorns arrived in Montana. Only a dozen years later, partners Tom Lynch and George Emerson moved one thousand head, the first large herd, north across the border to the Alberta range. The northern limit to the range of the plains bison, Alberta and Saskatchewan became the end of the trail for the Texas longhorn, the open-range cowboy and the chuckwagon.

An 1890s hillside campsite in Montana.
(Glenbow Archives NA-207-88)

There were few formalities around the chuckwagon in Montana in 1897.
(Glenbow Archives NA-207-72)

A chuckwagon bogged down at an innocent looking crossing at Rosebud Creek in 1921.
(Glenbow Archives NA-313-7)

stocking up

B y the middle of the century, the great open Canadian West was beginning to be seen as a frontier where fortunes could be made from other than fur trading. The lure of gold, the possibility of owning one's own land, and the advertisements lauding the possibilities of ranching gradually entered the minds of more and more people. Cattle drives that began in Texas and other parts of the American Southwest spilled over the border in growing numbers.

Although the majority of Canadian cattle drives took place on the eastern slope of the Rocky Mountains, they occurred first in British Columbia, and the longest drives travelled not north, but south. During the 1860s many small herds were trailed up through the British Columbia interior to supply meat-hungry gold miners in the Cariboo. Some of the more progressive drovers started ranches in the interior to provide a steady supply of beef. When the gold ran out, the only market for their stock was gone. This complication resulted in "one of the most notable [cattle drives] in the history of agriculture. Had it originated in Texas, the world would have heard about it in story and song." (MacEwan, 1975).

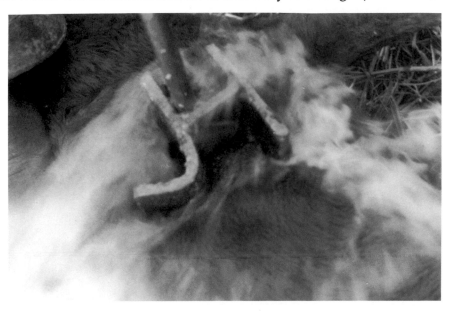

The Gang Ranch brand – JH for Jerome Harper – is one of British
Columbia's oldest brands. (Photo courtesy Hancock House Publications)

In May of 1876, Thaddeus Harper, founder of the huge Gang Ranch, started south from the Cariboo with a herd of heavy market animals. He intended to drive his cattle to the nearest

American railhead and ship them to Chicago. The 1 200 head moved slowly, taking all summer and fall to travel down to the border, through Washington, Oregon, Idaho and into northern Utah. While the cattle wintered, Harper received word of a cattle-killing drought in California. As soon as the animals were rested, he headed them west and the herd, cowboys and wagons rolled into San Francisco in February of 1878, 18 months and almost 3 200 kilometres (2 000 miles) later! During the 1870s and 1880s, European and eastern American investors were attracted by promotional material extolling the economics of ranching in the American West. It was said that ranchers could turn cheap cattle onto open range, pay a pittance for a few cowboys to mark the calves in the spring, then reap tremendous profits when the same hands gathered and marketed the fat stock in the fall, all the time increasing the size of their breeding herd at a phenomenal rate. Between roundups all but a few cowboys would be laid off and the investors didn't have to give a stray thought to the operation. Although the advertisements were grossly exaggerated, when the weather co-operated this laissez-faire form of corporate ranching did prove profitable – some netting 30 percent profits per year.

But ranching in the American West often proved a brutal and lawless struggle between cattlemen and other settlers. The relative peace on Canadian soil can be attributed to the firm and even-handed law and order provided by the North West Mounted Police from the time of their formation in 1873. In a paper presented to the Calgary Historical Society in the 1920s, pioneer rancher Fred Godsal pointed out that "the American cowboys shed their six-shooters at the boundary as the trees shed their leaves in the fall, and were glad to do so."

A quick bite under the shade of the chuckwagon's canvas. Notice the pistol worn by this Montana cowhand in the 1880s. (Glenbow Archives NA-207-107)

George Emerson and Tom Lynch had been trailing cattle from Montana into Canada since 1876. In 1879 they moved up a larger herd, 1 000 head, to stock their own ranch four miles west of present-day High River. Emerson knew that "Driving and selling won't always be good. Look at that grass beside the Highwood River. I never in all my days saw the beat of it – and but a few buffalo eating it."

Their stock wintered well on the nutritious Alberta grass and Emerson moved his operation farther south to Willow Creek, where cattle, horses and chuckwagons bearing his "Rocking P" brand ranged over foothills country for another quarter century.

Lynch continued trailing cattle and horses up from Montana for several more years before settling onto his TL Ranch on the north fork of the Upper Highwood. The TL chuckwagon led cattle to stock the North West Cattle Company ranch, which became the now-famous Bar U, as well as others including the Quorn, Mont Head, and Military Colonization Company ranches.

Pioneer cattleman George Emerson
(Museum of the Highwood 981-24-34)

The first western Canadian ranches were relatively small, owned by individuals, and they operated on the free grass principle; that is, they grazed their cattle on public land. When Matthew Cochrane, a Quebec senator and respected cattleman, decided to start a big ranch there was no policy concerning the open range grazing on crown land. Through his political connections he was instrumental in changing that situation.

Cattle owners from Central Canada and Great Britain added a touch of elegance to ranching in the Canadian West. The E.P. ranch house, c. 1923. H.R.H. The Prince of Wales walks towards the camera.
(Museum of the Highwood)

In 1881, the government instituted a grazing lease system in order to attract investment in ranching on a larger scale, and to control the use of crown land. This system, in which up to 100 000 acres could be leased for periods of up to 21 years at a rate of one cent per acre, encouraged large scale ranching indeed. By 1885, 46 leases totalling 1.7 million acres had been leased and stocked. Large ranching companies financed and managed in central Canada, Britain and the United States, soon dominated the industry.

Senator Cochrane took out the maximum lease on property he had scouted, west of the fledgling community of Calgary. Several colleagues acquired adjoining leases, boosting the Cochrane-controlled total to 190 000 acres. Duncan McEachren, the Dominion Government chief veterinary surgeon, became managing director for both the Cochrane Ranch and the Walrond, another maximum-sized operation. Senator Cochrane appointed former NWMP officer, Major James Walker, as his own local manager.

A Mountie visits the Bar U cowboys. Not only did the North West Mounted Police protect early ranching operations, many members left the force to become stockmen themselves. Cook Charlie Lehr sits on the wagon seat. Foreman Charlie McKinnon stands below (arms crossed). (McKinnon Family Collection)

To stock the new ranch, Walker travelled to Montana and purchased almost 7 000 head of mostly crossbred Black Angus, Hereford and Shorthorn cattle for $16 per head. I.G. Baker & Company, prominent Montana contractors, were to deliver the herd to the Cochrane's Big Hill headquarters for $2.50 per animal.

Because the drive started late in the season, 23-year old foreman Frank Strong divided the herd to speed its progress, each section with its own chuckwagon. The steers went ahead, travelling at 25 to 29 km (16 to 18 miles) per day, while the trailing cows and calves averaged 22 km (14 miles). Cowboys on drag "slickered and tin-canned" these cattle all the way (slapped lagging animals with slickers or ropes attached to stone-filled rattling tin cans). The hands kept the cattle moving so fast and bunched together so closely that they had little time to graze or rest. Young calves couldn't keep up. Tongue-lolling stragglers were loaded into trailing wagons. Once the wagons were full, exhausted calves were left to die, or were sold or traded to settlers for as little as a cup of tea or a glass of milk. Some cowboys preferred stronger drink in trade, and whiskey traders did a brisk business in Cochrane calves.

When the fast-moving herd reached the ranch, Major Walker could see that the cattle were in poor condition. He had the animals put directly out on the range – without taking time to brand them properly. Unfortunately, many of the emaciated creatures didn't have time to get accustomed to their new surroundings before the first snows fell. By spring roundup time, the coulees and draws of the Cochrane range reeked with rotting corpses.

Initially, many sympathetic locals helped the Cochrane cowboys gather their surviving stock. Dr. McEachren ordered every unmarked animal branded, and his order was followed, despite protests from neighbors who had animals in the same range. Walker's crew was abandoned as ranchers set off to brand their own animals before the Cochrane men could find them. They branded a few Cochrane cattle as well, in compensation for their own expected losses.

All the 21-year leases had contracted to stock their ranges to the maximum capacity – one animal per 10 acres – within three years. The Cochrane winter losses made it necessary to purchase more cattle. This time the drive was met by an early blizzard as they neared Calgary, but Walker insisted that they keep the animals moving and that the herd be delivered to Big Hill, as contracted.

Poindexter and Orr, the Montana ranchers leading the drive, gathered some local range steers and drove them ahead of the main herd to make a path through the deep snow for the exhausted cattle. On delivering the animals, a disgruntled Poindexter told Major Walker, "Here they are. You better count them now, because half of them will be dead tomorrow."

Dr. McEachren's orders now were to keep the animals on their own range, despite months of desperately cold, snowy weather, and despite the animals' attempts to struggle to snow-free grassland south and east of Calgary. Although most of the local ranch cattle came through this winter in fair condition, the Cochrane Ranch again suffered massive losses. Of approximately 11 000 head put out on the range over two years, only 4 000 were gathered in the spring 1883 roundup.

While the Cochrane operation floundered through its second year, other large ranches started up with much greater success. In May of 1882, Fred Stimson, manager of the North West Cattle Company, purchased 3 000 head of cattle at Lost River, Idaho, and hired experienced drover Tom Lynch to move the herd north. Lynch in turn hired a tall black cowboy named John Ware as cook's helper and nighthawk for the remuda. Ware had come to the northwest in 1879, on a cattle drive from Fort Worth, Texas, to Montana's Judith Basin.

Soon Lynch was impressed not only with Ware's riding ability, but also with the way he handled men and cattle. By the time the drive reached Helena, Montana, Ware was promoted from cook's helper to cowboy in charge of one section of the drive.

This North West Cattle Company herd safely reached the Highwood River, at Emerson and Lynch's former ranch site. Shortly after they arrived, the fall storm hit – the same storm that devastated the Cochrane Ranch herd. A bitter north wind swept across the open prairie

John and Mildred Ware on their front porch.
(Museum of the Highwood 967-10-6W)

and pushed the cattle many miles south. John Ware went missing along with the cattle. When the storm abated somewhat, Stimson and Lynch and their crew rode south, searching for him and for the herd. They found John Ware doggedly trying to keep the drifting cattle from reaching and re-crossing the Old Man River. Such devotion impressed Stimson. Ware was one of the few men kept on throughout the year, and he would remain on the Alberta range.

In 1883, a disappointed Matthew Cochrane decided that the country west of Calgary was not suited to cattle ranching and he and several friends acquired another huge tract of lease land (170 000 acres) in the Pincher Creek area. As they moved their remaining cattle south, a lanky Montana cowman named George Lane passed them. He was on his way north to become the new foreman of the North West Cattle Company.

One of Lane's first actions was to discontinue the use of the company's blotch-prone brand – a circle within a circle – and register the now famous Bar U brand. Under Lane's direction this great ranch would become home to top cowboys, renowned chuckwagon cooks, and huge herds of cattle and heavy horses. It was visited by royalty and outlaws alike, and has recently been designated a national historic site on the recommendation of the Historic Sites and Monuments Board of Canada.

The open range of the Alberta foothills was the epitome of cow country, and the chuckwagon became the image of the outfits that populated that vast rolling land with hardy beef cattle.

In 1883 George Lane, with $100 in his pocket, came to work for the North West Cattle Company. By the early 1900s he owned the operation (renamed the Bar U) and was running 40 000 head of cattle.
(Museum of the Highwood 967-5-2)

settling in

By 1883 the southern Alberta range boasted over 25 000 head of cattle, with more animals arriving every month. As the animals could spread out over many hundreds of square kilometres, and mingle with the herds of other ranches, ranchers found it necessary to organize large general roundups to gather the animals, separate those owned by each rancher or company, brand the new calves, and check for disease. In the spring of 1884, a large number of ranchers came together to round up their cattle.

The cattle populating western Canadian ranges in the 1890s showed a predominance of Shorthorn blood. (Bradley Collection, Museum of the Highwood)

Each ranch sent representatives, and each "rep" took six or more horses with him, as well as his saddle, bedroll, slicker and waterproof tarpaulin. (Some men took a tent, but most were prepared to sleep in the open.) Area ranchers grouped together, with one supplying the chuckwagon and the others paying "board." Men were known by their chuckwagon outfit, brand – such as the "Bar U boys" or the "Circle hands" – and although there was camaraderie around the chuckwagon campfire, the competition between wagons was legendary.

Each wagon crew followed the directions of their "wagon boss," usually the foreman at their ranch. As the roundup set out and progressed over many miles, a range boss was chosen, a man who knew that particular district or range well. Men followed orders and the roundup took on the organization of a military operation.

The 1884 roundup covered open range from Sheep Creek, not far south of Calgary, to the American border, from the slopes of the mountains to the prairies east of Lethbridge – most of it open grassland. Frederick Ings of the OH Ranch said that it took only one week to reach the furthest extent of the roundup range, but over two months to gather the cattle on the return journey. He described setting out:

> Once all the final preparations were made the cook would climb up onto the mess wagon seat and the night herder would go to the other. The four-horse teams would be harnessed and hooked to the tongues. A whip would crack. A shout would go up. With a strain of the tugs, the wheels would be in motion. We were off!

> The "Pilot," a man who was well up on the country, the trails and watering places, rode in front. The wagons would string out behind him, and after them the loose saddle horses herded together by riders in the rear.

> When the day's trail was ended, everyone helped to make camp. The tents were pitched and the wagons placed end-to-end. The corral ropes were fixed to the outside wheels of each wagon, ready to be put to instant use. "These rope corrals were our only means of catching our horses and were very necessary as the horses were turned loose to graze. Wranglers were in charge of these horses day and night." (Ings, 1980)

A roundup outfit moving camp in the Milk River area in 1912. Note the small stove cart behind the lead wagon. (Glenbow Archives NA-111-4)

Although they camped separately, cowboys from two or more wagons would work the range together. The roundup was hard work, from a hot meal at sun-up, to the last chores in the dark, as well as night herding on two-hour shifts throughout the night, no matter what the weather or terrain. Remembering one of the last large drives, in the 1920s, Stan Graber of the Matador Ranch in Saskatchewan, describes his role:

> The job of nighthawk meant I herded the remuda from dusk until daybreak and slept in the day – maybe – if I wasn't helping move camp or on a trail drive. When we got to the new camp I got out my bedroll and crawled under the bed wagon out of the sun, or for cover if it was raining. Someone else took care of the bed wagon horses to give me as much sleep as possible – there was always so much noise it was hard to sleep. It seemed like I was always tired.

The remuda had to be loose tethered [at night] so they could graze unhampered. It was my responsibility to continually check to see that no horses were missing. You couldn't count 125 horses in the dark, but there was a system that worked really well: horses are social animals, and a remuda of 125 head was made up of 10 or 15 cliques. One clique probably had a single white horse in it; another clique had two white horses; then there would be a bunch of all bays – which were hard to see in the dark – so you put a bell on one of them.

When it got wintery cold, as it often did in late fall while rounding up the beef herd, I would ride into camp a couple times in the night and curl up around the cookstove to get warm. I would eat the midnight lunch which the cook always made, and have some of the coffee warming on the back of the coal-fired stove.

Memories of nighthawking are of sitting on a grazing horse while somewhere nearby a coyote howled, of being cold and sleepy, and of solitude.

Montana in the 1890s. The night-hawk's all-night vigil with the re-muda re-quired that he get some sleep during the day. (Glenbow Archives NA-207-11 3)

But that big roundup of 1884 set the procedure that was followed for many years, as Ings explains:

When we were all gathered together, the range boss would give us his orders for the day. He would allot portions of the country to different men who, taking several riders with them, would work that part thoroughly, bringing all the cattle they found back to a common centre near the wagon. These were called circle rides and usually two were made in a day. At noon some riders were left in charge of the cattle gathered in the morning while the others ate lunch and changed horses, then the herders would be relieved to do the same.

After the second gather was accomplished the men would prepare the fires and the ground to work the latest batch of cattle. As the Bar U cattle were the most numerous, they were cut out first from each day's drive, branded, and turned loose; then another and another brand would be worked out until all the calves in that bunch had been gone over. (Ings, 1980)

Fred Ings described the task of catching a morning mount: "There would be the hiss of a lariat through the air and the loop would drop over a head. That was all the target we had, one head milling amongst a hundred others." (Glenbow Archives NB (H)-16-503)

"Circle riders" swept up scattered bunches of cattle and moved them to the main herd, collected near the next afternoon's chuckwagon camp. (Glenbow Archives NA-857-1)

Once the cattle were collected, unmarked calves were roped and dragged close to the fire where they were branded with their mother's brand. At the same time all the young animals might be inoculated and the bull calves would be castrated. (Bradley Collection, Museum of the Highwood)

As the cattle in each area were gathered and branded, the wagons and the growing herd moved to a new area and the process was repeated again and again, until they worked back to the area near today's Claresholm. There the wagons split up, taking their cattle back to their own districts, until each ranch had its own cattle back on its own leasehold.

> There were many rivers to cross, some swollen and swift. It was not easy to get the cattle into them and it required patience and skill, especially with calves. These little fellows would break back and had to be roped and dragged to the water. Men would have to herd the cattle as they swam with the current, to keep them from milling and turning back to shore. Often the horses would be swimming too. It was dangerous work for man and beast, but we made it across eventually and very few cattle were lost. Sometimes the newborn calves were carried along in a wagon; the mothers followed, bawling after them. Many calves were born along the trail. When they were a few days old they would trot along nicely with the others. (Ings, 1980)

Small streams like this one could become dangerous roaring torrents during the spring run-off. Drowning was second only to accidents involving horses in causing the deaths of cowboys. (Glenbow Archives NB (H)-16-493)

The next spring roundup in 1885 involved 500 horses, 100 riders and over 20 chuck- and bedroll wagons. It took two months to gather over 50 000 head of cattle. With that many chuckwagons on the job, you can bet there was considerable temptation for the cowboys to travel from wagon to wagon to check out the gastronomic specialties of the various cooks. The reputation of a large ranch often rested on the talents of its chuckwagon cook, and great tales were told of cooks' exploits, as much as those of the cowboys.

Ranching had certainly caught on in southern Alberta. Except for Cochrane's disasters, the industry thrived – until the winter of 1886-1887 provided a rude awakening.

Heavy snow fell in late October and continued until the middle of November. A warming Chinook blew in just long enough to melt a thick crust on the snow and then the wind shifted to the north and temperatures dropped down and down, eventually reaching -46 C (50 F below.) This glacial weather spilled across the great divide, reaching the ranches in the interior of B.C. and spreading south along the Rocky Mountains as far as Texas. Cattle suffered terribly, huddling,

> ... breast high in packed and crusted [snow] banks, dying as they stood; some who were sheltered somewhat by bluffs or coulees starved pitifully, ravenously searching for food until the frost had reached their vitals. The bodies of great steers were found in the spring, heaps of them, with their throats and stomachs punctured and torn by sharp splinters from dried and frozen branches and chunks of wood they had swallowed in their anguish ... The rabbits died, the lynx left, the herds of antelope starved in hundreds. (Kelly, 1913)

Breeding stock that had wintered on open range suffered less than the young animals just shipped from Manitoba or Ontario, which were used to barns and the provision of winter feed and water. Ninety to one hundred percent of these stocker-type cattle succumbed in that awful winter.

The spring roundup of 1887 gathered little more than half the cattle that had roamed the range the previous fall. Many American cattlemen were totally wiped out by the winter storms. Although losses were terrible, on the whole Alberta ranches fared as well as any in the west, better than most. The reality of ranching in the west was now painfully clear.

Mrs. Fred Ings of the OH ranch rides side-saddle as she turns cattle loose after a spring storm.
(Museum of the Highwood 967-10-6J)

# of cooks and cowboys

After the brutal winter of 1886-1887, the huge general roundups were replaced by smaller regional affairs, to which small operators continued to send reps. While a rep for a small rancher named Goldfinch, young Lachlin McKinnon discovered there were precise regulations concerning roundup reps. Although McKinnon and his horses had travelled thirty miles from Goldfinch's home base to the Little Bow, "the roundup boss headed me straight back for home with orders not to come back unless I was properly equipped with the right number of horses [he was short two] as well as with the money necessary to pay the roundup fees."

On the roundup everyone and everything was treated fairly. "All livestock was of equal status and any rider would care for any animal in need, regardless of who the owner might be." (Lachlin McKinnon, Pioneer, 1950). If it was the cowboy's duty to treat all cattle equally, it was the chuckwagon cook's job to do the same for the men. Although cooks often had a tough reputation – "only a fool argues with a skunk, a mule, or a cook" – their worth was certainly recognized by ranch managers. During the hey-day of open range ranching, if a top cowpuncher made forty dollars a month, the cook would make fifty, only ten dollars less than the wagon boss.

Members of the Stoney and Blackfoot tribes knew the range as well as any white man. Two Indian cowboys pose with well-known bronc buster Frank Ricks.
(Museum of the Highwood 967-10-6L)

The chuckwagon cook had to be a man of many talents: capable teamster to handle four often-bronky horses or mules and look after their tack; doctor for the cowboys and sometimes veterinarian, using remedies from his "possibles" drawer, or a needle and thread to stitch man, horse, harness or clothes; camp engineer; diplomat; and of course resourceful chef to make meals quickly with whatever limited provisions and equipment fit into the back of his wagon.

And the cook had to be durable. Like the cowboys he served, the cook carried on seven days a week, for weeks on end, until the roundup or drive was over.

In 1890, Oscar Brewster [of the 101 Ranch in Oklahoma] is supposed to have set the open prairie record of cooking three meals a day for as many as 85 hands for a period of 21 days.

During that time, using Dutch ovens, Brewster asserts, "I served hot biscuits, all they could eat, at every meal." (Renno, 1982)

Rarely was there leisure time for the cowboys, or the cook, to sit around the campfire in the evening, telling tales. After a hard day in the saddle, the cowboys were "plumb happy just to go to bed at night," especially since they would soon have to get up for a night herding shift.

Cooks came in all sizes, all colors and all personalities. Some of the more notable included German-born Charlie Lehr who worked for the Bar U from 1887 to

His shirt sleeves rolled up on a warm day, cook Charlie Lehr airs out the cook tent. (Glenbow Archives NA-466-22)

1899, and was "remembered by the old timers as one of the best natured of the roundup cooks. He never pulled out without seeing that the wagon, harness and grub were all in order for the trail. His meals were on time and his camp set in the right place." (Leaves from the Medicine Tree, 1960) In direct contrast to Lehr's reputation were some fellows whose nicknames told it all, men like "Dirty Dick," "Old Poison" Finlay, or another fellow to avoid, known simply as "Death on the Trail."

Perhaps a storm has forced these Bar U hands to take shelter in Charlie Lehr's cook tent. (McKinnon Family Colllection)

Many other cooks were known for their culinary specialties. Billie Grier and the Matador cook Jim Hayes were both noted as sourdough experts; Ed Larkin made top-notch raisin pies; "Mulligan" Jack Thomas, as well as building a fine Irish stew, created the distinctively named dessert, "Son-of-a-gun-in-a-sack."

Lachlin McKinnon remembered that some of the chuckwagons supplied more and better supplies than others. He recalled a wagon run by two men named Shattuck and Dancy:

> To start out they made liberal quantities of good jam available to the riders. It seemed to disappear very rapidly, however, so they started holding the jam back, only to be served in case visitors happened along. W.W. Brown, "Brownie," was a very witty character and used to be the life of the camp. Whenever a strange rider or anyone driving a team headed toward our camp, Brownie would call for the cook to "bring out the jam, we are going to have company!"

Conditions for keeping food were difficult, and each cook had his own tricks of the trade. On cold nights some took their sourdough starter into their bedrolls, to keep that crucial ingredient for bread "alive." Bert Sheppard of Longview explained that the Bar U cowboys he rode with ate a lot of beef. In order to keep the meat above the range of blowflies, the cook hung a quarter, like a flag, from a long pole attached to a wheel on the bed wagon or chuckwagon. Neil McKinnon recalls that the LK Ranch cook stuffed eggs inside the oat barrel where they stayed cool and well cushioned from shell-cracking shocks.

Sourdough biscuits in the making. In Montana there are batches of sourdough starter tracing their lineage back to the chuckwagon cooks of the 1800s. (Bradley Collection, Museum of the Highwood)

Billy "Forks" Houston of the 76 received his nickname after he angrily tossed the pointy utensils at his balky mule team and left his outfit short of forks for the rest of the roundup. Other well-known cooks included "Frenchie" Ouimet, Willie Andrews, Harry Hayes, "Mexican" John, Jack Emsley, and Fred Anderson of the Oxley, who brought part of the chuckwagon right into the ranch house kitchen by laying a wagon wheel on the dining room table to create a lazy Susan spinning server.

Cooks were often the butt of jokes or pranks. On one mange-dip roundup a big cowboy named Jack Morton had several run-ins with the chuckwagon cook, Louis-Joe. It seems that Morton, who was late for supper one eveing, upset the cook so much that he left the cowhand nothing to eat. Morton would have gone to bed hungry if John Ware had not shared his meal. The next morning, breakfast was late because Morton had hidden the cook's pants. A few days later the cook "accidentally" spilled hot coffee in Morton's lap.

The affair would have continued but the cowboy wisely decided to postpone his revenge until the last day of the dipping. After the boys had finished their last meal and Louis-Joe was cleaning up, Jack surveyed the cook and shook his head. "You have us worried," he said, "at all the itching and scratching you've been doing lately. We figure you must have contracted a dose of the mange."

With that he wrapped his long arms around Louis-Joe, lifted and carried the

Mange dip channels were filled with up to two metres (six feet) of a steaming hot, vile smelling mixture of lime and sulphur.
(Glenbow Archives NB (H)-16-466)

frantically struggling cook toward the dipping vat. He held him for a moment, suspended over the dirty, foul-smelling trench; it was littered with hair and dirt from thousands of head of cattle. Then he dropped him. As the spluttering chuckwagon cook splashed and scrabbled out of six feet of liquid, Morton ventured the comment that one dip should be enough to rid the cook of his itch.

The space between the chuck-wagon and the cooking fire was sacred ground – the cook's private domain. Cowboy etiquette declared that the men hold back until the cook gave the signal to "Come and get it!" At the call, the hands didn't wait to be served, they just helped themselves and then sat down to eat wherever there was an open spot. Seconds were allowed only after everyone had "firsts."

Around chuckwagon camps personal privacy was respected. If a stranger rode in he was welcome to stay for a meal, but if he didn't offer his name, he was never asked. A man hired on with an outfit was asked "what shall we call you?" and only a first name, or even a nickname, sufficed. A man was judged by his present actions – his past was his own worry.

Spencer brothers roundup wagon in the Milk River area. Cook Jack Berry wearing the apron.
(Glenbow Archives NA-777-2)

There were ways to find out about a man's background. After one incident on the Saskatchewan plains, there was no doubt in the cook's mind that cowboy Jim Spratt was American-born. Upon being told that the pot held tea rather than coffee, newcomer Spratt shot the pot full of holes and threatened the cook with the same fate if there weren't coffee for breakfast. There was coffee for breakfast, and the crew knew that Spratt wasn't a Britisher.

Sometimes the hands became upset with one another's chuckwagon manners. One crew was annoyed with a wrangler who continually raided the cook's raisin box, which nestled just in front of the chuckbox on the wagon. One morning a cowboy replaced the raisin box with a similar one containing fresh cow manure. Everyone around camp watched as the young rider eased his horse over against the wagon, reached down into the wagon, and jerked back a dripping, green-brown hand.

With women in camp, some men might remove their hats during a meal, but wearing one's hat wasn't considered disrespectful in 1901. Neither was exchanging hats for a photo session!
(Bradley Collection, Museum of the Highwood)

Women weren't a common sight on a roundup, but if they arrived for a visit, or occasionally to help out, they were treated with the greatest respect.

Early Canadian cowboys dressed remarkably well on the range – white shirts, vests, and often ties as well. Handkerchiefs proved useful, not only for a throat wrap or dust mask, but also as rancher Fred Godsal described – to strain "wrigglies" out of stagnant prairie ponds in order to get a drink. Cowboys used various methods for laundering their meagre wardrobes. Some washed their clothes in streams, taking care to pound the seams with rocks to crush the lice. Others were known to place the dirty items on top of an anthill where the diligent little insects picked the woven cloth clean and ferreted the lice out of the seams as well – an environmentally friendly dry-cleaning and delousing operation.

If a cowboy were going to see a lady, he took extra care to clean himself as well. William and Susan Brown were early settlers near Queenstown, Alberta. Mrs. Brown was noted for her fine meals and hospitality, as well as for her five lovely daughters. Their home became a mecca for lonely range riders from the Circle and other nearby ranches. Before arriving at the house, cowboys washed off accumulated dust at a small body of water that still bears the name "Slick-Up" Lake.

Although the cook was usually employed year round, at the end of the fall roundup only a few trusted men were kept around to feed and keep an eye on the cattle until spring. Some of the unemployed cowboys drifted to town to pick up work at a livery stable or tending bar. Others rode the "grub line," travelling from ranch to ranch and staying a week or so at each, doing odd jobs in exchange for food and a bunk. Their visits were usually welcomed. At a time when there were no telephones, the grub line riders carried the latest news, mail or messages from ranch to ranch.

Although it was difficult to stay well-groomed on the range, personal hygiene became important when a cowboy planned a trip to town.
(Glenbow Archives NA-777-21)

The rigors of living outside in all kinds of weather meant that it didn't take long for range hands to get old and stove up. If a fellow hadn't saved enough to buy his own place, or worked up to a manager's position by the time he was 40, he would likely have to find a less strenuous occupation, sometimes as a chuckwagon cook. Some of the cooks eventually acquired places of their own. The Bar U's Charlie Lehr took out a homestead near a spring that had been a favorite camp site for his chuckwagon outfit.

Louey Hong enjoyed working as cook for Pat Burns. But after two years of moving camp all the time and spending his summer months bumping on a chuckwagon seat across southern Alberta, he decided to settle down. Hong purchased the general store in Cluny where he soon became the most successful and popular merchant in town. His store could certainly hold more than his chuckwagon, and he boasted it even carried more stuff than The Hudson's Bay Company.

6

end of the open range

Chuckwagon use depended entirely on the open range style of ranching and the need to carry all the necessities of life for as long as trail drive or round up lasted.

As the vast grasslands were fenced, the need for general round ups and the cowboys' mobile kitchen began to disappear. In a pattern similar to the American example, where large ranches purchased wire and staples by the boxcar, it was the large outfits that were first to do extensive fencing to keep the "scrub" bulls of settlers and small ranchers away from their breeding stock. In 1885, in an attempt to improve their breeding program, the southern branch of the Cochrane Ranch strung the first large barbed wire fence in Alberta, a 25-mile barrier along its northern boundary.

Railway lines were another barrier to cattle, as well as a source of sparks that ignited range-destroying grass fires.

But many other barriers forced the closure of the open range cattle industry. No longer could cattle be turned loose and only rounded up twice a year for branding or marketing. The 21-year leases were expiring and ranchers had to "alter the capital basis of the industry from cattle to land." (Breen, 1983) Government land surveys divided the range into 160-acre parcels which disregarded availability of water or other land-use features, forcing ranchers to buy all the land that their cattle required for grazing and watering.

Cattle left to fend for themselves on the open range were at the mercy of the weather. (Glenbow Archives NA-2245-1)

Mange mites were a growing problem faced by open-range ranchers. During the late 1800s and early 1900s, to defeat the infestation all the cattle on southern Alberta rangeland had to be gathered and immersed in dipping vats filled with a bubbling, vile-smelling mixture of lime and sulphur.

Roundup statistics for the Rosebud area in the summer of 1903 showed the dipping vats to have been used to treat a 100 000 head of range and farm cattle. (MacEwan, 1983)

An incident that dealt the final death blow to the old style of open range ranching was the terrible winter of 1906-1907, exactly twenty years after the killing winter of 1896-1897 (see Chapter 4).

In the fall, prairie fires burned off winter pasture. The cold weather and snow came early and hard. Late fall blizzards drove unsheltered cattle south and east until they piled against fences or into coulees where they froze. Ranchers, such as the McKinnons of the LK, who had learned from experience, put up winter feed and their animals survived reasonably well, but many lost huge numbers of their herds.

The Gardners of Pirmez Creek, west of Calgary, had just moved their herd east to the Hand Hills. Both their winter pasture and hay stacks were burned by the hot, dry summer's grass fires, and they lost sixty percent of their stock over the winter. Jack Morton at Gleichen bought feed wherever he could find it, then used free-running horses to trample the snow so his cattle could reach the purchased hay.

Riding past rotting corpses made the spring roundup of 1907 a bitter affair. For many cattlemen it was the end of their ranching careers. With fewer experienced hands available, ranchers became frustrated at trying to keep up the spring and fall roundups.

> The roundup became more and more complicated as the farmers began to increase their small herds. Often they came to help gather herds, mounted bareback on a plow horse wearing a blind bridle, with a couple of mongrel dogs running and yelping in every direction. As a rule these fellows were far more of a nuisance than a use. (Lachlin McKinnon, Pioneer, 1950)

Longtime cowboy and chuckwagon cook Stone Roberts noticed a deterioration in the quality of riders. In the early 1920s he was cooking for the Bar U, the largest spread and one of the last to continue the spring and fall roundups. Roberts turned to another oldtimer, indicated one youngster and shook his head. "I opened a box of prunes this morning and

This chuckwagon at the Knee Hill roundup around 1910 has seen better days. (Glenbow Archives NA-1062-6)

that kid came out of the box. The rest," he indicated the others, "are from Eaton's." (Leaves from the Medicine Tree, 1960)

What with the encroachment of settlers, the cutting up of range into smaller and smaller portions by railroads and a growing spiderweb of irrigation ditches, "when the [LK] roundup wagon pulled in as a full unit in the fall of 1909, it was for the last time. It was never put out again and this sounded one more note in the death knell of the fast expiring open range era." (McKinnon, 1979).

Gradually all these barriers combined until the days of the open range were over.

Reports of 80 to 90 bushel-per-acre yields attracted many newcomers to southern Alberta. Ill-advised government policies, however, placed many unfortunate settlers on dryland farms which would have been better left to cattle. (Museum of the Highwood 967-144-103)

With the end of the open range, instead of riding for months on spring and fall roundups, much of the time cowboys and their horses were kept busy cutting and stacking winter feed.
(Museum of the Highwood 978-56-14)

off the range, onto the racetrack

Although the open range life of the western cattle industry lasted only a generation or two, it became ingrained into the North American personality. Many mourned its loss, none more so than a young man from Rochester, New York. He ran away from home, travelling west to learn to rope and ride, but ended up plying his trade in Wild West shows instead of the now-fenced range.

Tall, lanky Guy Weadick was more than just a promoter. He wasn't afraid to get inside a corral and work with a bronc. (Bradley Collection, Museum of the Highwood)

On two visits to southern Alberta – in 1904 as bulldogging announcer for Bill Pickett's show and in 1908 with Miller Brothers' 101 Ranch Show – young Guy Weadick was impressed with the people and the western atmosphere. He saw Calgary as ideal for his dream, a spectacular frontier celebration. Weadick discussed his dream with Canadian Pacific Railway official, H.C. McMullen, a former cowboy and trail hand who had followed a chuckwagon into Alberta in the late 1870s. McMullen liked Weadick's idea, but advised waiting. Two years later Weadick approached the Calgary Industrial Exhibition manager, E.L. Richardson who also liked the idea, but balked at the $60 000 price tag. The brash and enthusiastic Weadick then approached ranchers George Lane, Patrick Burns, Alfred E. Cross, and Archibald J. Mclean who agreed to finance the Calgary Stampede with $100,000, $40,000 more than the original budget.

Calgarians supported Weadick's 1912 show. On Labor Day, September 2nd, thousands of mounted Indians decked in heavily beaded buckskins led the two-mile long opening parade. Behind them, western Canadian history continued to unfold: Hudson's Bay Company traders in axle-screeching Red River carts, followed by pioneer missionaries in buggies; whiskey traders and their nemesis, the red-coated Mounties; then the early cowboys and ranchers – either mounted or riding atop battered chuckwagons, and pioneer farmers aboard their white-canvassed prairie schooners. At the rear were cadres of Labor Day-celebrating workers. Viewers lined the streets or crowded onto balconies and rooftops.

By advertising $20,000 in prize money and World Championship titles, Weadick attracted visitors and participants from across Canada and the United States. A group of vaqueros even travelled north from Pancho Villa's Mexico to compete in the roping events at "the Greatest Show of the Age." Although rainy weather ensured that neither the "Big Four" nor Weadick reaped great profits, the event was still considered a success.

Weadick and his wife Flores La Due, a trick rider and roper, returned to Calgary in 1919 to produce a Victory Stampede amidst the euphoric atmosphere following the end of the First World War. But he could not convince promoters to support an annual event until 1922, when E.L. Richardson decided that partnership with Weadick's Stampede might revive his flagging Calgary Industrial Exhibition.

Immediately following his appointment as Stampede Manager, at a salary of $5,000 – the same wage as the city of Calgary's mayor – Weadick put his promotional skills to work.

Calgary's first Stampede in 1912 featured stagecoach races. These top-heavy vehicles tipped easily and were difficult to repair or replace. (Museum of the Highwood 979-15-62)

Trail rides at his Stampede Ranch west of Longview provided a relaxing diversion for Guy Weadick and his paying guests. (Museum of the Highwood 967-57-17)

In one evening 11 108 people enjoyed barbecued buffalo sandwiches at the 1923 Calgary Stampede. (Glenbow Archives NA-3985-16)

His persuasive letters secured the participation of many "big names" of the day. The heir to the British throne, the Prince of Wales, who had purchased a ranch in 1919 just south of Weadick's own spread, agreed to donate a trophy to the 1923 Saddle Bronc champion; Canadian actress Mary Pickford and her husband Douglas Fairbanks awarded trophies for the Roman Standing Race and the Relay Race; local businesses such as the Great West Saddlery and Riley and McCormick contributed trophy saddles.

The 1923 Calgary Exhibition and Stampede would "pay tribute to the pioneer cattlemen of the North West." In his promotional material Weadick wrote:

> Calgary will really turn back to the good old days for one glorious week. Citizens will wear cowboy attire and the main streets will be reserved during the mornings for saddle horses, Indian Cayuses, chuck-wagons, cowboys, and cowgirls. (Weadick Promotion)

The show was to kick off with "a stupendous parade on Monday morning" and end on Saturday night with a barbecue of "buffalo meat cooked in deep pits over a roaring fire." To entertain the grandstand crowd, Weadick introduced new events – the wild horse race; the wild cow milking contest; Indian races – including an Indian Slow Race, in which the *last* horse to lope across the finish line won – all topped off by a spectacular fireworks display. But the new evening competition that unexpectedly captured public attention was Event No. 10, the "Cowboy's Chuck-Wagon Race."

> Primitive, rattling, lumbering, range-scarred, mess wagons fully equipped. Their daring drivers on the swaying seats handling the ribbons on the fastest four-horse team their ranch can produce. Old-timers who know no fear, and daredevil young 'uns' desperately pitting their skill in racing rivalries. They break camp, load their wagons, cut a figure eight around two barrels, and run a half mile on the track to finish under the wire in just under two minutes . . . The mad glories of the chariot races of the Roman Coliseum eclipsed by the rangemen of the west. (Weadick Promotion)

The pitting of one chuckwagon against another in a race was certainly not a Weadick original. Many an impromptu competition involved outfits vying for first choice at the next evening's campsite. The earliest written account of such a race stated:

> About 1892, four wagons were camped together on the Walrond range. They were moving to a new campsite and all got away at about the same time. Each cook was anxious to get the best campsite and it developed into a race over rough country. The Walrond manager, Doc Frields, cut in and pulled his wagon out, not wishing to see it wrecked. One of the other wagons lost their stove, and the Punkin Roller's door to the mess box came down and all their utensils were scattered over the hillside. (Leaves from the Medicine Tree, 1960)

When Weadick contacted local ranchers to enter their wagons in an organized race, many declined, but he convinced a half-dozen to compete. Rather than have all six wagons on the track at once, Weadick divided them into two heats of three outfits each. This required that each wagon's running time be noted, to decide the day's winners. In the Prize List and Rules for *"Stampede" A Romping Rangeland Rumpus,* the entry for the 1923 wagon races took only a few lines.

```
┌─────────────────────────────────────┐
│  ┌───────────────────────────────┐  │
│  │      EVENT NO. 10. –          │  │
│  │   COWBOYS' CHUCK-WAGON RACE    │  │
│  │   PURSES AND PRIZES $275.00    │  │
│  └───────────────────────────────┘  │
└─────────────────────────────────────┘
```

Day Money

First $25.00

Second $15.00

Third $10.00

FREE ENTRANCE

Man entering team that wins the greatest number of races out of 5 will be awarded a special prize of a $25.00 John B. Stetson hat.

Rules

1. This is for Official Canadian Championship title.

2. Three or more to start each day. Each outfit to consist of four horse team, wagon, driver, and four helpers. Team hitched up to start. Cut figure eight around barrels, out through backstretch into track, run around track back to camp bround [sic], unhook team from wagon, stretch fly. No less than two stakes, and make fire. First smoke decides winner.

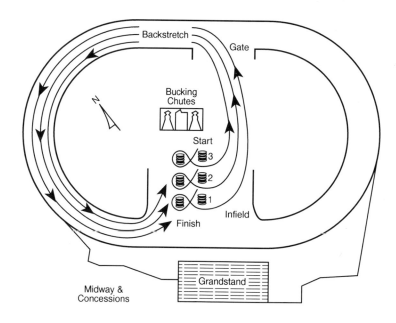

The first races involved fully-loaded chuckwagons which followed the illustrated route before returning to their starting barrel positions to set up a new camp. (Illustration by Brent Lowrie)

On June 30, 1923, the *Calgary Herald* stated that the new "chuck-wagon" race,

> promises to be one of the most thrilling and entertaining on the program . . . various individual ranches and districts represented will turn out the complete round-up outfit . . . The wagons will carry the real range equipment, such as chuck box, tent, branding iron . . . all the paraphernalia used on a regular range wagon.

Four of the six entries were pool wagons organized in a similar fashion to those assembled by local ranchers to gather cattle on the open range. These four were the Sheep Creek wagon entered by Jack Butler and Ora De Mille; the Kew or Double Dishpan outfit entered by Bob Carry, the Hodgkins brothers and driver Sid Bannerman; the Lewis and Shore outfit from Langdon driven by Lloyd Lewis; and the Mosquito Creek wagon backed by ranchers Dan Riley, A.E. Cross, Jack Drumheller and Rod Macleay, driven by Bill "Sourdough" Sommers, a veteran longline skinner who once drove the Dawson-Whitehorse stagecoach.

The last two of the six outfits were driver-owner rigs: Jack Morton's CX outfit from Gleichen, and Clem Gardner's V Quarter Circle from Pirmez Creek.

Art Hudson, a member of the Mosquito Creek outfit, worked for A.E. Cross' A7 Ranch in 1923, and later remembered that their two lead horses were the cart horses the A7 used to run errands back and forth to town – "a well-broke, quiet team," but that they could "get to town and back in a hurry." The wheel team came from Dan Riley's ranch, noted as grade animals that loved "to run in the harness." The vehicle was a 3½, a heavy wagon that would be too much for the thoroughbreds racing today, but "duck soup" for the A7-Riley team to pull empty. The other equine participants were an assorted lot, some Clydesdales, some half-breeds, and some horses said to have "some breeding."

The horses are unhooked. The tent pegs are in place. A competitor signals for time as the smoke rises from his stove, around 1923 or 1924. (Dillon Collection, Calgary Exhibition and Stampede)

That first July 9th evening, as the lumbering chuckwagons rumbled onto the track, pots and pans clanking and dusty canvases flapping in the breeze, they were pacesetters. Their wagon wheels traced a figure eight path around the infield and out onto the racetrack that chuckwagon drivers would follow from that day forth.

During the first race Clem Gardner's V Quarter Circle rig came in with the fastest time – 3 minutes and 15 seconds, but the *Calgary Herald* reported that "the judges disqualified them [Gardner's outfit] because they had failed to turn first in front of the grandstand before making the smoke." (Calgary Herald, July 10, 1923). As has occurred so often since then, the first outfit across the finish line was not to be the winner. The Mosquito Creek wagon crossed second, but were awarded first night honors for their penalty-free time of 3 minutes, 45½ seconds. The "helpers" (now called "outriders") following Bill Sommers' winning wagon were Bill Livingstone, Dunc Fraser, Slim Sonnie and Laurel Miller.

Art Hudson remembered, "There was something wrong with every race we ran. There were meetings going on every night in every barn." Hudson said that George Lane and A.E. Cross helped drivers and organizers adapt and work out new rules for chuckwagon racing.

One rule was drafted after the Mosquito Creek wagon outriders whipped their own chuckwagon horses just as "Sourdough" Sommers was trying to turn the outfit from the track into the infield. The wagon tipped onto its side. The next day, the judges instituted a rule forbidding outriders from "helping," or interfering with their driver once a race had started.

Upsets like this have been a part of the game since the inception of chuckwagon racing.
Note the rare number five barrel from 1924.
(Dillon Collection, Calgary Exhibition and Stampede)

Mrs. Elizabeth Bell claimed that after this incident, a disgusted Bill Sommers stepped down from the chuckwagon, threw the lines to her husband Joe Bell, and said, "Here, you take the buggers. I'm too old for this game." Art Hudson also claimed to have driven the Mosquito Creek outfit in 1923. With all the uncertainties surrounding a new event and the lack of early record-keeping, it is possible that two or three different men drove the wagon on different evenings of this first meet.

J.B. Cross outrode for the Mosquito Creek rig in 1924, the second year of the wagon races at Calgary.

> The wagons lined up with their cook stove and fly all in the wagons. They started around the race track doing a figure eight which was not very well arranged to start with, being very unfair to the first and second wagons . . . Our first wagon horses . . . could run a little faster than I could, but not much.
>
> After going around the track you were to end up at your original barrel. All wagons . . . were supplied with a good set of brakes. The outriders were to grab the reins of the horses so they could be unhooked . . . and brought round to the side of the wagon. The stove was on the side of the wagon to start . . . the old way of having wagons on the original round-ups. This stove was taken around to the back and the fire was started . . . to show that you had finished the race. Unfortunately, a lot of people got the stoves undone and got the fire going quicker than the people could undo the horses. So there was consider-able confusion in the first year as to which thing happened first – and therefore as to who won.
>
> The other confusing thing was that the wagons were unable to stop at their own barrel, crashed into another wagon which was probably stopped properly, and there was complete confusion – great excitement for the spectators. The second year . . . the horses were not unhooked when the wagon got to the final stopping place. The horses were to stop, the fly and stove were taken off, the stove [with two lengths of stovepipe attached] was lit . . . Your smoke signalled that you had finished the race . . . (Interview with J.B. Cross, n.d., Glenbow Archives)

After five days of racing at that first 1923 meet, the *Calgary Herald* stated that on Saturday, July 14, "Dan Riley of High River, Alberta [and his Mosquito Creek outfit] won the largest number of chuck wagon races and . . . received a Stetson hat." (the *Calgary Herald*, July 16, 1923). Whether Sommers, Bell, Hudson, or all three drove the winning wagon in 1923, and whether organized chuckwagon races had been run in other venues before Calgary, are moot points now. The Mosquito Creek outfit was declared the winner and it was Guy Weadick who brought this exciting new racing event, the Rangeland Derby, to public attention and acclaim.

In 1924 the wagons circled an altered figure eight pattern that brought them out onto the track directly in front of the grandstand, then circled the half-mile track. At the start of the race, to preserve open range authenticity, the outriders not holding the lead horses were to be "seated, as in camp, around the stove" at the back of the wagon. At the end of the race the wagons were to stop in the infield and light their "camp" fire.

The 10 wagons that entered the 1924 show were divided into two heats of five. Watching 40 horses and 25 men race around the barrels and the track proved a spectacular attraction that thrilled spectators and organizers alike. Other problems arose. Ranchers accustomed to doling out "a bucket of oats and a few forkfuls of hay that didn't cost anything at the ranch," found that the cost of horse feed in the big city added up to more than the prize money. Not wanting to lose their popular new event, Stampede officials agreed to supply the chuckwagon outfits with feed, a policy which continued for 40 years.

Running on Stampede hay and oats, the Mosquito Creek outfit, driven by Art Hudson, completed the fastest time of the 1924 meet by raising smoke in less than two minutes. Tom Lauder of Huxley had the fastest aggregate time, however, and his Bagley and Lauder rig won the 1924 "chuck-wagon races" at the Calgary Exhibition and Stampede.

Faster times, tighter rules – chuckwagon racing was an established fact.

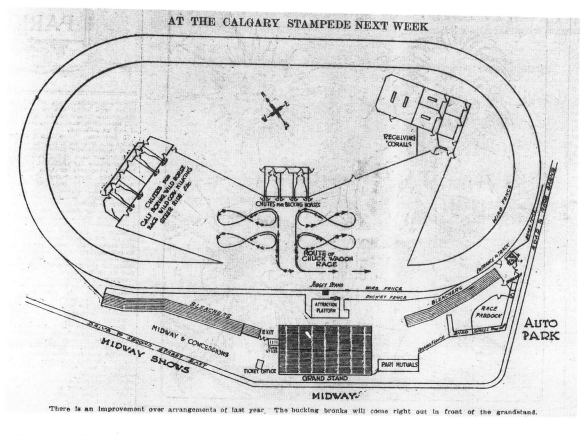

If a race had ever been run in this fashion, disaster would have been the inevitable result! The Calgary Albertan's illustrator obviously misunderstood the 1924 race organizers' intentions, and had the chuckwagons circling their barrels on the horizontal instead of the vertical. (Glenbow Library)

Chuck Wagon Race
Calgary Stampede No 64

The scramble to unhook and unload the wagon and raise smoke at the end of a race could be both dangerous and anticlimactic. In 1925 the rules were amended to recognize the first wagon to cross the finish line.
(Cosgrave Family Collection)

pace setters

The early years of chuckwagon racing were populated by characters who have become part of the history and legend of the sport. Clem Gardner, Jack Morton and Tom Lauder had a lot in common, but were very different personalities.

In 1923 when Stampede Manager Guy Weadick challenged local ranchers to enter an outfit in the first "official" chuckwagon races, Clem Gardner signed up his V Quarter Circle wagon and placed among the top three finishers every night of the meet.

Gardner's experience with wagons and horses began early. He was only an infant when he travelled 1 000 km (600 miles) as his parents moved from Russell, Manitoba, to Pirmez Creek, southwest of Calgary. From the time he was old enough to crawl into a saddle, Gardner played, then worked with horses, learning to ride and rope while handling stock in open range round ups.

In 1906, Captain Gardner decided to expand the family operation by sending 500 head of cattle to the Hand Hills. Clem, his older brother Teddy and sister Minnie loaded their chuckwagon and trailed the cattle 150 miles to the new spread north of the Red Deer River. They spent the awful winter of '06 - '07 there, gathered what few were left of their herd in the spring, reloaded their chuckwagon and trailed the survivors back to their home place.

Young Clem Gardner became so proficient a bronc rider and steer roper that he was declared Canadian All-Round Champion Cowboy at the 1912 Calgary Stampede. Several years after racing began, Gardner and Johnny Van Wezel from Strathmore introduced thoroughbred race horses to the chuckwagon track.

Clem Gardner truly was an all-around cowboy, riding and winning in the saddle bronc, steer roping and chuckwagon events. (Glenbow Museum NA-1942-4)

Clem Gardner's Calgary Stampede quarter circle wagon poses with Guy Weadick (mounted, front

With those faster horses on his team Gardner won the big show in 1931, and his wagon provided continuous tough competition until 1936, when he retired. For many years Gardner supplied cows, calves, steers and bucking horse stock for the Calgary Stampede. He and his daughters trailed up to 300 head from their ranch, across the Elbow River, over to the Victoria Park rodeo grounds. During the Depression, the Stampede livestock contract

ight) and the 1923 winning Mosquito Creek outfit, driven by Art Hudson, c. 1924. (Dillon Collection, Calgary Exhibition and Stampede)

provided ready cash that helped keep Gardner's and others' ranching operations afloat and allowed many to continue wagon racing.

In 1952, at the Stampede's fortieth anniversary, Clem Gardner received an illuminated scroll declaring him the 1912 contestant who had contributed "the most to the growth and success of the Stampede."

Clem Gardner and Johnny Van Wezel introduced lighter, faster, thoroughbreds to the chuckwagon track. (Glenbow Museum NA-1241-898)

Like Clem Gardner, who had a foot on both the range and the racetrack, Jack Morton had eaten many a meal cooked on the back of a chuckwagon. At one time Morton was said to be Alberta's largest mixed farmer, counting his cattle, horses and cultivated acres in the thousands.

Jack Morton's outfits ready to begin seeding in southern Alberta. At various times Morton owned the CX, Pacific Cold Storage, Two Bar, and Indian Springs ranches. (Glenbow Museum NA-4119-1)

Chuckwagon competitors were originally required to enter at least one other rodeo event. Often they chose the Wild Horse Race. (Dillon Collection, Calgary Exhibition and Stampede)

Morton used his own field operations and hired hands to train new draft animals. Once a horse had a few hours in harness, Morton considered it "broke" and often sold the animal to an unsuspecting buyer, on the spot.

Raymond Bragg, who drove a seed drill on one Morton farm, claimed, "Horses were coming and going like guests at a country hotel . . . we never drove the same horses two days in succession." Using half-trained horsepower had its drawbacks. One inexperienced hand, unwilling to admit that he could not stop his unruly team, drove up and down a field for most of a day without refilling his seeder! But Morton was full of contradictions, and could also be generous to a fault; he was known to give desperately poor farmers not only draft horses to work their fields, but the harness as well.

In 1919, at the Gleichen rodeo, Jack competed in the Wild Horse Race on the team of another chuckwagon racing original, Tom Lauder. Morton was to grab the head of the animal while Lauder saddled and mounted the animal. In this race, now legendary in its retelling, Jack held on, even when the horse's front hoof caught in his belt and peeled his trousers to his knees, leaving the ladies in the audience utterly shocked. Their team won the race.

Most observers would have described the first chuckwagon races not as sport, but as a spectacle or performance of ranching lore. "Sundown" Jack Morton certainly put on a performance. His unpredictable nature was perfectly suited to the early wild-and-wooly stage of chuckwagon racing.

Jack Morton put on a good show, even away from the rodeo grounds. Here Morton (left) sits on a trick horse while stroking his tame badger.
(Glenbow Museum NA-4121-2)

Jack Morton, riding behind his chuckwagon, signals his crew to move up closer in a 1923 parade. (Glenbow Museum NA-4006-9)

When Weadick asked Morton to run in the planned chuckwagon races, Morton agreed, providing there weren't too many rules. There weren't, and if there were any shortcuts, Morton found them. In order to speed the fire-making at the end of the race, Morton soaked his wood in coal oil. As he tossed in the lighted match, the stove exploded, blew off its lids and spooked the tied-up horses. Even so, the gas fire didn't produce the required smoke.

Morton carried two "tame" badgers as mascots on his chuckwagon in the opening day parade, and later in the week he and his crew initiated the first chuckwagon breakfasts on downdown Calgary streets. Although he didn't win the 1923 races, he captured the attention of the spectators and the media. In 1924, the *Calgary Herald* recorded Morton's return:

> Big Jack Morton from the Circle C camped at Chestermere Lake last night en route to the city. Morton has with him a chuckwagon, a democrat, two California carts, a dozen cowboys and a big herd of bucking horses. they plan to whoop it into the city in great style this morning.

A victorious Tom Lauder waves to the grandstand crowds. (Glass Family Collection)

With his pet badgers beside him, Morton's outfit won prizes awarded to "the outfit which excelled in authenticity and condition of old time equipment, and its cook's efficiency in preparing flapjacks and other typical roundup food" and the "best all around driver." He was a grandstander, a born show off whose pranks were sometimes dangerous to himself, bystanders, his crew, and his horses. However, his showmanship was the stuff that Weadick loved to give his audiences, and the audiences loved Morton's antics.

Morton retired from chuckwagon racing with a flourish on the muddy track of 1938. While his wagon was turning the barrels, the pole snapped. With the wagon whipping from side to side, he found it impossible to pull up his team, so he just whooped and hollered at the horses until the jagged end stabbed deep into the ground, hurling wagon and driver high into the air. Johnny McNab remembered that the point jabbed a full four feet into the muck – so far that the track crew had to hitch up a work team to pull it out.

Despite the severity of the wreck Morton only suffered a broken arm. He was riding a horse within days, and less than a week later he cut off the cast.

Morton's earlier Wild Horse Race partner, Tom Lauder, not only contributed to the lore and lure of early chuckwagon racing, but he also began the first chuckwagon racing dynasty, now in its fourth generation.

When Tom Lauder was only nine, he was riding race horses around Dodd's Lake on the old Innisfail racetrack. He competed in the 1912 and 1919 Calgary Stampedes and entered the democrat races at the 1923 Calgary Exhibition and Stampede, finishing second for the week. But what really caught his interest was the new "chuck-wagon" race.

The first chuckwagon race prize was a $25 Stetson hat. Here, Tom Lauder proudly displays the 1924 trophy.
(Glass Family Collection)

The next year Lauder and Ray Bagley put together an outfit, with Lauder driving. They warmed up the week before Calgary by winning the first-ever chuckwagon racemeet at Crossfield, Alberta, and then, using the same team of Red, Dan, Judy and Blaze, Lauder duplicated his Crossfield win at the Calgary Exhibition and Stampede. The Bagley and Lauder rig rattled off the fastest aggregate time after five days of racing, the new rule for determining the big winner.

Like Morton, Lauder had a knack for circumventing the few regulations that did exist and this proved a catalyst for new rules. Rather than completing the full figure eight, some drivers turned their outfits directly only to the track. The judges assigned a one-second penalty to deter offenders. Lauder quickly figured out that the advantage gained more than made up for the penalty, and continued ignoring the full figure eight turn, until the penalties were increased to a sufficient deterrent of ten seconds per barrel missed. In the meantime, he set a track record with his shortcut that remained unbroken for many years.

During the 1925 races Lauder's outfit flipped a full somersault after hitting a barrel. Actor and movie producer Hoot Gibson was on hand filming "The Calgary Stampede," but no camera was rolling and the actor lamented that he would have given anything to catch the spectacular accident on film. Lauder got Gibson to name a figure for a repeat performance. With $200 stuffed in his pocket, Lauder performed the dangerous stunt again. He made more money from that one act than if he had won the Stampede championship.

Lauder repeated his earlier Stampede win in 1927 and 1928, but there wasn't much money to be made from prizes. In order to pay expenses, Lauder and other early drivers also trailed strings of up to fifty bucking broncs as they travelled from show to show, receiving $8 for an ordinary bucker, and from $25 to $100 for one that put on a money-winning show. Until 1927, bronc riders had to sit their mounts until they quit bucking. Many top broncs were tamed after being ridden to the finish a few times, so rodeo committees were always looking for replacements. Some of the top names in the bucking world, Tombstone, Grave Digger, Cyclone, Shimmy Shaker, No No Nora and Home Wrecker, were at one time or another in these wagon men's strings.

In the mid-1920s, Lauder and his broncs travelled east with Peter Welsh's show, the Alberta Stampede. On this trip, Lauder's left arm was nearly ripped off by the horn of an angry bull. The doctors wanted to finish the job, but he refused, and made his way home caring for the injury himself. His own doctor agreed not to amputate and treated the wound. By the next year Tom was driving again, but the injury redirected the blood supply so that he no longer had a discernible pulse in his wrist. Whenever Lauder required medical care from then on, he enjoyed watching the reaction of nurses as they searched his left arm for signs of life.

Tom and Goldie Lauder settled near Huxley in the 1930s, to run the Lone Star ranch. A five-pointed star brand graced their chuckwagon and their cattle. They raised five sons and three daughters just as chuckwagon- and horse-crazy as their father. The younger girls, Iris and Babe, tended to overshadow their older married sister. At one gymkhana Iris and Babe were winning all the events, until a young woman named Kaye Jensen finally beat them at the stake race. The fellow presenting the awards was delighted when young Mrs. Jensen stepped up to receive her award. "I'm sure pleased to give a prize to someone other than a Lauder," he said. The young woman looked disappointed. "I'm sorry, sir," she apologized, "but I'm a Lauder too." Kaye Jensen was the older married sister.

Jack Lauder with his father's Lone Star outfit. (Glass Family Collection)

In the late 1930s, Lauder suffered 13 broken bones and the loss of a fingertip after his wagon tipped coming off the barrels. From then on, Goldie could no longer watch the barrel turns when her family members were driving.

"Poor Mom," remarked Iris [Lauder] Glass. "First she had Dad, then Bob was an outrider, then Jack started driving and outriding, then Bill and Jim too. I married a wagon man and so did Babe [Ralph Buzzard]. Mom's life just kept rolling, wagons, wagons, wagons, and it never quit for her, ever. She even saw our son Tom drive."

When Tom Lauder turned the driving lines over to son Jack in the early 1940s, at least Goldie didn't have to worry about her husband racing any more; she didn't have to worry about him speeding on the highway either. He never did trust motorized vehicles. If he did have to drive a car, he never travelled over twenty-five miles an hour. Tom Lauder liked to go fast, but only as fast as four good horses could run.

These old-timers – Gardner, Morton and Lauder – helped form the style and thrills of chuckwagon racing, as the wagons moved into a new phase of their history.

Tom Lauder (left) rides in the Calgary Stampede parade with other "old-timers."
(Kaye Jensen Collection)

the transitional years

The image of the early years of chuckwagon racing is of those larger-than-life characters driving big heavy wagons pulled by big heavy horses, and following very few rules. As the popularity of the wagon races grew and racing circuits developed and expanded, the sport became more organized, and certainly more safety-conscious for the drivers, the outriders and particularly for the horses.

The wagons changed. By the end of the decade much of the original paraphernalia was stripped away. Most wagons no longer carried the traditional water barrel and tool kit, few sported brakes. Even the namesake chuck box was only bolted into the back of the wagon to add authenticity for parades. Horse gear was reduced from heavy working harness to a light buggy design, little more than a pair of leather trace-tugs attached to hames and a collar.

Although the equipment was stripped down for speed, Johnny McNab insisted that he and the other outriders competed just for the fun of it. "There wasn't the kind of money up then," McNab explained, "There wasn't as much incentive to win, so we just had a darned good time. Not that the fellows didn't try to come in first. Boy, some of those drivers were wicked with their whips. We outriders had to bury our faces in our horse's mane; otherwise a whip-happy driver might wrap his lash around our necks."

Every penny was needed in the thirties and none of the drivers made a living at chuckwagon racing. Even a top competitor like Dick Cosgrave needed farm income and an assistant arena director's wage to keep bread on the table.

The popularity of wagon races encouraged the creation of other shows which sprang up all around Calgary – Strathmore, Black Diamond, Millarville, Crossfield and Midnapore, and then gradually spread further afield to places like Pine Lake, Lacombe, Innisfail, Didsbury, Sundre, Chestermere Lake, Trochu, Three Hills, Content, Delburne and Lousana, throughout central and southern Alberta.

Long-time wagon men like Jim Ross, Sid Bannerman, Theo Thage and the Hamilton brothers, also trailed bucking stock behind their racing outfit. As well as providing steady income, some broncs were also used as spare harness horses. Jack Higgins bucked a top bronc named Blizzard in the afternoons and drove the same horse on his chuckwagon at night. The times were too tough to accommodate freeloaders. At the end of racing season, top chuckwagon horses often pulled hay rakes or binders, or chased cattle.

During the season, the moving of all the stock, wagons and supplies was a major production.

The early racing wagons came straight in from the range. Pulled by heavy horses, they carried all the traditional equipment. (Dillon Collection, Calgary Exhibition and Stampede)

The length of early whips is clearly evident in this 1939 race photograph. Notice the old Calgary Stampede barns. (Glenbow Museum NA-1241-883)

A team of work horses pulled the chuckwagon that carried our food, supplies and equipment. The chuckwagon horses were tied behind and the bucking horses just followed along . . . At night we would stop, set up camp and cook something over the campfire. We would string ropes between the fences across the road allowance to make an enclosure for the animals. (Through the Years, 1980)

Lowen's chuckwagon at the community picnic, Taylor's flat, Drumheller area in the late 1930s. (Glenbow Museum NA-4186-21)

The expanding chuckwagon racing circuits encouraged new riders and drivers to try their hand at the sport. Most rodeo competitors in the thirties were men who had grown up riding and driving horses. Many drivers and outriders were still working cowboys. A number of Indian competitors joined the sport then, including Slim McMaster, Tom Jerry and Dick White Elk of Gleichen, Frank Medicine Shield of Cluny, the Tsuu T'ina's (Sarcee) David Crowchild, Tom Simeon of Morley, and Johnny Lefthand from Eden Valley.

Some early outriders didn't stay long with the wagons, but proved successful in other fields. Jim Brown followed Slim Swain's outfit for several seasons before joining CFCW in Camrose, Alberta. He became the dean of Canadian Rodeo Broadcasters and remained a loyal supporter of chuckwagon racing throughout his radio career.

Wilf Carter rodeoed and outrode in the late twenties, before deciding it was easier to make a living strumming his guitar as "Montana Slim."

During the evenings, after the races were over, Wilf Carter would come over to our camp and perch up on Jim [Ross'] wagon, play his guitar and sing long into the night. People would stop and listen and we would soon have a large crowd around our campfire. (Through the Years, 1980)

There was even a real blue blood who raced an outriding horse around the Calgary track. Fred Percival followed Harry Brogden's DeWinton outfit and later, as the Earl of Egmont, settled down on the Two Dot ranch, west of Nanton.

Drivers also moved through this transitional period. Some got hooked, but others moved on. Johnny Van Wezel of Strathmore set a new track record of 1 minute, 12.25 seconds in 1936. The Goettler and Hamilton families

In the early years of chuckwagon racing, competitors often trailed bucking stock for hire. This bronc was part of Dale Flett's string. (Dale Flett Collection)

from DeWinton raced two winning outfits in the thirties; their Sheep Creek outfit won with Eben Bremner driving in 1934, and again in 1939 with top horseman Sam Johnson on board. Jim Ross always had a superb turning and running outfit, capturing Calgary in 1925, 1929 and 1932.

Western music and street dancing have been featured since the first Calgary Stampede in the 1920s.
(Bradley Collection, Museum of the Highwood)

It was during the 1930s that the more competetive drivers started hiring men who excelled in their outriding positions. Bill Hamilton contended that Johnny McNab was the best stove man in the business. "Those old stoves were quite a weight, seventy-five pounds, but Johnny got under them and loaded them with his knee. Many drivers appreciated McNab's ability and on many evenings he rode and threw stove for more than one outfit. McNab himself gave a lot of the credit to good horses, especially praising a big bay gelding named Rambler, who always "stood like a rock" behind him.

During the thirties many new rules were introduced. In 1936, the Calgary Stampede began to require outfits to wear matching shirts to help both the judges and the audience identify each wagon crew. This regulation resulted in a blossoming of colorful gear, with the men wearing matching shirts, scarves, pants and hats. Outriders who followed more than one wagon in an evening began to dress with one shirt on top of the other, stripping off each outer layer as the races proceeded. Johnny McNab was dubbed "Mr. Many Shirts."

Sometimes, even with matching shirts, it was difficult to tell who was who. McNab remembered the dust being "God-awful thick" racing down the backstretch into the setting sun, and being barely able to make out the ears on his own horse, let alone see the horses and wagons around him. He remembered one race in Trochu, where the dust billowed so thick that a terrified driver abandoned his wagon by leaping into the infield.

Running in difficult conditions in an already spectacularly-dangerous race played havoc with men's nerves. DeWinton's Bill Hamilton declared, "After so long it got to you. You couldn't cut it anymore. That's why we quit. Some of the fellows," he added, "they got by a little longer with a couple shots of whiskey – some drank a whole bottle before they crawled up on the wagon."

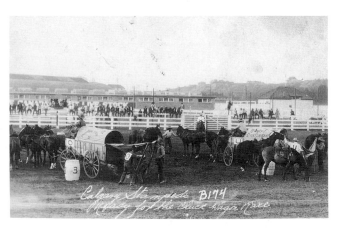

Outriders for Johnny Van Wezel and Dick Cosgrave prepare for the start of a race in the 1930s.
(Bradley Collection, Museum of the Highwood)

Most competitors confined their drinking to a few bottles of beer after the races were over. But even that indiscretion was often concealed. Bill Hamilton's wife Ruth was the daughter of top driver Sam Johnson. Ruth remembered that her father kept a ledger, "and when he came home here was all this money down for 'orange crush.' Mother and I never saw an orange crush bottle," but she did notice a lot of other long-necked brown bottles around the barn.

Some women travelled the circuit, but very few were involved with the training and care of the horses. Females excelled out on the track, however. Sheep Creek's winning rig in 1939 featured three distaff members – Beaut and Patsy Lewis on lead and three-year old May matched on the wheel with one lucky male, Sharky. The mares on that winning outfit pulled a much sleeker wagon on a much safer track than what Dick Cosgrave's team pulled nine years earlier, at the beginning of the transitional 1930s.

Dick Cosgrave won ten world chuckwagon championships and retired to become arena director for the Calgary Stampede. He and his crew sported matching blue shirts, red neckerchiefs and white pants. (Glenbow Archives NA-1241-920)

Problems with dust were not confined to the early days of chuckwagon racing, as this 1982 photo shows.
(Targhee Photo by Gordon Biblow)

Despite a broken rear axle, Sam Johnson leads Dick Cosgrave in the final turn.
(Cosgrave Family Collection)

dynasties

Chuckwagon racing, perhaps more than any other sport, is a family affair. Often several generations, men and women, boys and girls, work in the wagon barns caring for horses and cleaning and repairing tack. They travel together in the mobile home that replaced the chuckwagon as the "home on the range." It is also common for young men to follow their fathers, fathers-in-law, uncles, even grandfathers, and great-grandfathers onto the track. But each wagon family was begun by someone who got hooked on the sport.

Dick Cosgrave's grandfather was among the six jury members who convicted, but recommended mercy for Louis Riel. Dick's father, William (Pat) was ranch instructor for the North Blackfoot Reserve near Gleichen, where the budding wagon racer was born in 1905.

A stocky teenager, Cosgrave "wanted to become a world champion bronc rider and if he had pursued his ambitions along this line, he would in all probability have starved to death," instead he "found his niche in the world famous chuckwagon race." (Kennedy, 1952) In 1926, the second year he drove a chuckwagon, Cosgrave raced to victory at the Calgary Stampede. Two years later, in Guy Weadick's movie "His Destiny," Dick was the stand-in, or perhaps more appropriately, sit-in driver for Hollywood cowboy star, Neal Hart.

Dick Cosgrave on Wild Boy. (Calgary Exhibition and Stampede)

He resumed his winning ways at Calgary in 1930 and became the second man, after Tom Lauder, to win Calgary twice and qualify to keep the Silver Spray Brewing Company's silver urn. Cosgrave won again in 1933, missed 1934, then collected an impressive four straight victories, from 1935 to 1938.

His was not always the fastest outfit, but Cosgrave avoided hitting barrels and his well-schooled and conditioned animals ran consistently.

He provided top mounts for his outriders and, in exchange for equally top wages, he expected absolute loyalty – no "many shirts" on his crew. His men seldom made mistakes and usually finished each race so close to the wagon that "you could toss a blanket over them." This was important in the early days when the penalty for late outriders was assessed at the discretion of the judges.

Neal Hart looks down at Guy Weadick, who is pointing to the villain in this publicity still from the move "His Destiny." Johnny Van Wezel's Strathmore Roundup rig was one of many wagons used in that 1927 film. (Bradley Collection, Museum of the Highwood)

Cosgrave's wagon carried a water barrel on the side for many years, and his canvas retained the distinctive boxy shape reminiscent of an old round-up chuckwagon.

In 1935, he married Olive Flett, daughter of pioneer rancher and noted horseman, Les [Pop] Flett. Olive Cosgrave's brothers Elmer, Marvin, Orval, and Dale Flett would all excel as outriders or wagon drivers, and when Cosgrave became Calgary Stampede "straw boss," Pop made sure the Cosgrave operation ran smoothly. Marvin Flett trained the Cosgrave horses as well as his own Buckhorn Ranch outfit. His wagons consistently beat Cosgrave's when practicing at home, but when they got to the racetracks Cosgrave always managed to get his name on the trophy.

In 1939 Banff sculptor Charlie Beil was commissioned by the Canadian Western Natural Gas Company to produce a new trophy, a bronze replica of a chuckwagon. To keep this extraordinary work of art, a driver had to win the Calgary Stampede three times. By then Dick Cosgrave had already won the show seven times, but those earlier victories didn't count. He won again in 1940, missed in 1941, and was ready to give it another try in 1942, when his barn and most of his horses were destroyed in a devastating fire.

Cosgrave didn't give up. Borrowing horses from his fiercest competitors, including Brave Knight from Jim Ross and Beaut from Gene Goettler, he won the 1942 show. He needed one more victory at Calgary to own the Gas Company Trophy. Dick and Olive were so confident that they built a place for it into their new stone fireplace.

During the 1943 Stampede, Dick's outfit broke and rebroke the Calgary track record. But on the last night of the show, outrider mistakes marred his remarkable exhibition. His wagon crossed the finish line with both pegs and the tent fly dragging. Cosgrave's lead over the second place Johnson & Higgins wagon was less than three seconds. Controversy raged over the penalties to be assessed. Finally, Cosgrave was declared winner. Dick and Olive proudly placed the bronze in its fireplace niche.

That gave Dick Cosgrave a total of ten Calgary Stampede championships, a feat never equalled. The only driver to come close was his brother-in-law Dale Flett.

Flett started as an outrider behind his brother Marvin's wagon. Pushing his horse, Dollar Bill, to be first, outrider Dale would cut between Marvin's turning wagon and the top barrel and race out onto the track ahead of the outfit. These stunts annoyed Marvin. The brothers continually argued about racing tactics, and when Dale criticized Marvin for not avoiding a wreck which cost their outfit the 1945 Stampede championship, Marvin challenged Dale to do better himself.

Dale trained four young horses, Flash, Ranger, Scout and Betty, and within two years the team was turning and running with the best. Flett claimed a special gift for handling horses. "Horses and me got along from when I was a kid. If you ever saw me with them you'd know that I can do things with horses that others can't."

Lloyd Nelson recalled how Flett's outfits worked. "Dale's team had to be one of the very best. They drove and turned like a well-oiled machine. You couldn't pick one horse out as being exceptional – the whole outfit worked well."

Flett rarely turned actual barrels when he practiced, but spent hours cutting figure eights in the field. "I want them going by the lines, not by watching the barrels," he explained. "So they drive where I want them to go." Once on the racetrack he relied on instinct to turn the barrels. "When your outfit's working, you don't have time to think," he explained. "You just do it."

Despite injuries that would plague his career, and force his retirement, by 1956 when he began racing full time, Flett had perfected a formula for victory that won him seven of the next eleven Calgary Stampede titles. He took calculated risks on the track, but left nothing to chance with his equipment, horses or outriders. His horses were always parade-slick and gleaming; his harness and tack well oiled, and his red and yellow wagon in perfect running order.

By the time he retired in 1969, Dale Flett had gathered quite a collection of trophies. (Dale Flett Collection)

Although in racing trim, Flett's horses usually carried more flesh than most of his opponents' animals. This extra weight gave them more "bottom" for running a grueling six-day Stampede, and Flett often beat the other big names. One of his outriders was his nephew, Bobby Cosgrave.

Dick and Olive's son Bobby had been a precocious child who drove a pony chuckwagon outfit in the old Calgary arena when he was only 14. He drove big wagons at the Stampede two years later, but not with his father's blessing.

"I started outriding for my uncle Dale Flett when I was sixteen," Bob explained. "I wanted to build a wagon outfit then too, but Dad wouldn't let me, so Dale built one for me. One old horse of Dale's, Pepper, was as fine a leader as I ever hooked up. I drove Dale's horses for two or three years before Dad got mad and said, 'If you're determined to drive we better go buy an outfit.'"

They bought four young horses, all related. "I hauled hay and fed the cows all winter with that bunch, and by spring they were broke. I drove them four years before I changed a horse . . . Nowadays these guys hook something different every night, but back then if you had to change a horse you damn near cried."

As Bob Cosgrave's wagon circled the track, particularly down the homestretch, he would bounce up and down on the wagon seat. Country and Western singer Wilf Carter, perched on a bale in the Cosgrave barn, wrote a catchy tune that immortalized "Bouncing Bobby." Ruth Hamilton always wondered "how much faster those horses would run if Bobby'd just sit still."

Wilf Carter sings "Bouncing Bobby" for the first time. (Cosgrave Family Collection)

In 1967 Bouncing Bobby won the Calgary Stampede with his uncle Dale's Flett Brothers outfit. Two years later Bob won again with his own outfit, sponsored by antique dealer John Irwin.

Bob's wife Bernice, busy raising the children, and cooking for the crew, never did get involved with training horses. "I don't like horses and cows," she stated emphatically, "and they don't like me. I would clean the barn though, as long as the horses were outside."

Bernice became a color commentator, working at various times with all the well-known race announcers: Bill Cameron, Stan Sparling, Henry Viney, Lorne Ball, Jimmy Hughes,

Robin Ingram, and finally with CFCN's Ken Newans. Her daughter, Robin Gist, has followed her mother's lead, working with CFAC radio.

Bob and Bernice's oldest child, Richard, the third generation, spent all his spare time around the wagon barns. Allen Brown and Eddie Wiesner, outrider-drivers working for the Cosgraves, were well-known pranksters. Late one afternoon, they lifted young Richard and slipped the back of his belt over a heavy spike used for hanging harness.

"They hung him there and came for dinner," said Bernice. "I was looking all over for Richard before I heard his yelling, and found him out in the barn, hanging from his belt."

"I fired those two then and there," she said. "But when I couldn't get Richard down myself, I had to hire them back."

Only nine when he jockeyed his first race, Richard was twelve the first time he outrode, for Allen Brown at Morris, Manitoba. Richard was still too small to reach the saddle horn to swing onto his outriding horse, so he grabbed the saddle strings and jumped. Brown remembered that the boy was, "late every race, but at least he was a rider; there was nobody else."

Richard outrode next at the Meadow Lake Homecoming Stampede in 1971, for Hally Walgenbach and for me. He and I were both riding for Walgenbach in the final heat. Bernice was announcing, and informed the grandstand crowd that her son Richard was the youngest outrider on the track, only 14.

Richard turned away, kicked the dirt and began cursing. I led my horse over to ask what was wrong.

"Goddammit," Richard exploded. "I wish she'd kept quiet. Now everyone knows how old I am and I won't be able to get into the bar tonight."

Since he was knee-high to a thoroughbred, Richard had ridden on the wagon with his father in the practice turn before each race and in the post-race grandstand parade. At a benefit meet in Stettler, Bob asked, "Do you want to drive?"

Richard had been driving pony chuckwagons for several years, but never the big ones. "Sure!"

Bernice was judging that evening. Much to her surprise and horror, after Bob made the practice turn, he handed the lines to Richard, and hopped off the wagon to hold the leaders for his son's first race.

The lad was running against World Champion driver Tom Dorchester and Stettler's Bob Baird. After the horn blew Richard made it around the barrels and onto the track, but as he later explained with a grin, "Tom outran me by 30 wagon lengths. I never ate so much dust in all my life."

Early in his career Richard Cosgrave developed an aversion to hitting barrels – he seldom hits one even when practicing. He has another aversion, to brushing horses, and has an arrangement with his family that if he avoids one, he can avoid the other as well.

"At Morris he hit a barrel," Richard's wife Tara laughed, "and everybody came to watch him brush. It was the first barrel he'd hit in two years."

When Richard married Tara Glass, they blended the genes of two of chuckwagon racing's most illustrious families. Their children are growing up in the barns too, fourth generation on both sides.

Tara's mother, Iris Glass, travelled from show to show with her parents Tom and Goldie Lauder, sleeping under the wagon or in tent camps, cooking meals on the same stove that was tossed into the back of the family racing chuckwagon.

After the onset of WWII, Tom Lauder set up a drayage business in Dawson Creek, BC, supply centre for construction of the Alaska Highway. Seventeen-year-old Iris drove a team of horses, hauling supplies from the rail depot to the town stores.

Iris' older brother Jack had preceded his family to Dawson, accompanied by a young man named Ron Glass who ferried fuel for the highway construction. Glass was a strapping big fellow who could single-handedly load and unload 45-gallon drums weighing 205 kg (four hundred and fifty pounds).

Iris had already seen Glass' skill with horses when in 1931, at 15 years of age, he had replaced an injured competitor and driven a chuckwagon at the Calgary Stampede. He had driven throughout the 1930s, on one occasion driving five outfits in one night. Iris Lauder and Ron Glass impressed each other sufficiently that they were married after returning to southern Alberta in 1945.

Ron Glass and Jack Lauder got everything loaded into Armandine. (Glass Family Collection)

The newlyweds and their truck, Armandine, a three-ton surplus Ford truck named for the company title stencilled on the door, returned to the chuckwagon business. Ron recruited a half-standardbred horse named Peanuts from his father's Bowness dairy farm; his partner was appropriately named Popcorn. Glass purchased another top lead team, Casey and Gay Lady from 1944 champion driver, Theo Thage.

In 1946, a rambunctious wheeler kicked the front out of the Glass wagon box. Ron and Iris had barely enough cash to get Armandine from one show to another, let alone buy lumber to fix the wagon. Armandine was rumbling down a prairie road toward the next show at Wainwright, when fate intervened.

At a deserted intersection Ronnie noticed a fallen dead-end sign leaning against its post. "My God," he said. "That'd make a great front end for our wagon."

At Wainwright, he replaced the broken front end with the sign. Iris was so impressed with the black and white design, that, instead of covering it, she painted the rest of the wagon box to match the checkerboard! Soon they were using the distinctive design on their wagons, team shirts, water buckets and horse blankets.

With two excellent lead teams Glass won the Calgary Stampede three times in the late 1940s, becoming the second driver to capture the coveted Charlie Beil trophy. His streak of victories continued through the 1950s, winning three circuit championships for his long-time sponsor, Johnny Phelan.

Casey and Gay Lady were such quick starters that most stove men couldn't do their job. One frustrated outrider insisted that the task was impossible – no human could throw a 34 kg (seventy-five pound) stove to land in the stove rack once those horses began to move. When Glass bet that he could throw the stove at least the necessary 6 metres (20 feet), the outrider just laughed.

Glass paced off the distance behind the wagon's stove rack. The outrider stood at the back of the wagon, his hand casually resting on the endgate. Glass crouched over the stove, lifted and heaved. The stove travelled so far that it smashed against the endgate, and the outrider's fingers, before dropping into the stove rack.

Glass claimed he was in the horse business, not the wagon business. For many years he dealt away his well-trained lead and wheel teams to drivers with deeper pockets than his own. "There's always more horses, and you're only ever offered a good price for one once. If you don't take it something'll happen to the horse. He'll get colic, or caught up in wire during the winter, and you'll never get a chance to sell him again."

Iris disagreed. "There's been hundreds and hundreds of horses through our harness, "she said, shaking her head sadly, "and I fought over every one that went."

Bobby Cosgrave, who bought quite a few horses from them over the years, maintained that Iris would be so upset that it was almost dangerous to enter the Glass barn to retrieve his purchases.

Iris played an important role with their horses. Not only did she train and groom them, but she often rode them in the afternoon flat and standing Roman races, and also drove teams in the two-horse cart races. Occasionally she took four lines in her hands and drove the chuckwagon outfit in practice runs, but never in a race, feeling that she was "just not strong enough to handle four big horses."

Iris Glass has taken on every task around the wagons. This time the woman behind the men took the lines herself. (Glass Family Collection)

Like other wagon kids, Tara and Tom Glass helped with the chores.
(Glass Family Collection)

Ronnie and Iris's four children all played an active role in the family operation. Sons Reg, Tom and Rod all competed as outriders, with Tom riding for Bill Greenwood's winning outfit when he was 15.

Father and son on a practice run. (Doug Nelson photo, Museum of the Highwood)

Rod, the youngest, was killed in 1971 while outriding, in a tragic accident on the Calgary track. The family carried on for the rest of the week, but in the years following the tragedy, Ron Glass lost the desire to drive.

Tom bought a number of horses at his father's retirement auction, including a big bay wheeler named Opey, and a sorrel leader called Mexico. Father and mother continued to travel the show circuit with Tom.

Tom Glass drove his own black and white checkerboard wagon to the 1980 "Battle of the Giants" at High River and the WPCA circuit championship for Gulf Canada. He won the circuit championship again in 1981, shortly before his father Ron passed away.

Iris continued to travel the circuit with her son. At the Regina Buffalo Days Tom's right hand leader horse, Swing Leader, started ducking, or turning too soon on the top barrel. Iris suggested a technique Ron had devised to cure a horse of that habit.

Tom had run very well at earlier shows, so the announcer was praising his driving skills as Glass headed his team in for their practice turn. Even the announcer gasped an amazed "Oooh!" when Tom swung his horses left at the top barrel instead of right. The trick worked, and an equally amazed Swing Leader quit ducking.

Tom emulated the achievements of his father and grandfather by winning the Calgary Stampede in 1983 and again in 1987. That year Tom's son, 16-year old Jason, followed in his dad's tracks by outriding behind a Stampede-winning outfit his first year out.

When Jason Glass decided to start driving in 1989, the family built him a chuckwagon for a Christmas present. The box was finished and primed with four coats of white paint when Iris asked Tom if he felt it was ready for the checkers. Tom hesitated. He suggested they wait to ask Jason if he might want some other color.

Iris exclaimed, "Over my dead body he will!" and the checkers were painted on.

Jason loved his present.

Two great lead teams race to the wire: L.O. Nelson's Duke and Eugene, and Tom Dorchester's Blondie and Bigshot. (Nelson Family Collection)

During the 1990 season he drove his Mullen Transport outfit well enough to qualify for a position at the 1991 Calgary Stampede, where he became the fourth generation of the Lauder-Glass family to drive on the Calgary track, and the third generation to sit atop the famous checkerboard.

One of the other drivers to qualify for the 1991 Calgary Stampede was Dallas Dorchester.

The Dorchester dynasty began in the 1940s, with eleven-year-old Tom sitting on his pony watching the horse races at Wetaskiwin. A horse threw its jockey on its way to the track for a half-mile race. The rider refused to remount and the owner asked Tom to ride. The boy readily agreed. As he mounted, Tom saw his father coming and figured the game was up. But his father gave permission, advising "Hang on tight and don't kick the horse with your heels."

Young Dorchester followed Dad's advice and rode the horse to victory that day and the next. He competed in, and won, relay races, chariot races and one of his favorites, the standing Roman race. In that event, two horses run side by side with the rider standing above them, balancing one foot on either horse. When the Calgary Stampede included

Roman races in 1944, Dorchester won both days. The same year he competed successfully as an outrider for the winning outfit driven by Halkirk's Theo Thage.

Eventually Dorchester decided to try handling four horses. In 1948 he purchased a small sorrel mare named Blondie from chuckwagon driver Ralph Innocent. Blondie is considered by many old-timers to be the best barrel horse ever to wear harness. She would crouch almost on her belly to gain purchase as she turned round the barrels. Dorchester drove Blondie on lead with a stallion named Bigshot, who had to scramble to keep up with her. Because Blondie put so much effort into the start and turn, she had little energy for the end of the race. But the advantage she gave made up for her lack of "finish." Very few outfits ever beat Blondie and Bigshot to the track. The pair epitomized Tom Dorchester's belief that a race was won or lost in the first seconds.

"You have to get around those barrels as quick as you can," he insisted. "If you can make it to the rail first then the other guys have to go around you; they have to run two or three seconds faster to beat you."

Dorchester's outfits were tough to beat from any barrel position, but they were especially dangerous coming off the short number three or four barrels. While many cursed their luck when they drew a short barrel, he rubbed his hands with glee. After the horn sounded, he would cut a quick figure eight and be first on the track. Blondie and Bigshot usually captured the rail position cleanly, but if not, the canny Dorchester would make use of his forward location to squeeze and intimidate the inside drivers and their lead horses. This often resulted in the other outfit hesitating enough for Tom's wagon to slip onto the rail.

Sponsored by Jack Sheckter, he ran well through the 1950s and into the 1960s, never winning a championship, but consistently placing in the top five at Calgary and on the professional circuit. Bigshot died in a trucking accident, but Blondie continued to run until 1964 when the eighteen-year-old mare led Dorchester's wagon to a second place circuit finish.

Late that season Dorchester, his wife Joy and their oldest son Garry headed east with Cliff Claggett's touring show. When Tom offered to let Garry use Blondie on his wagon, the young man hesitated, "I was scared of hurting her."

Garry did drive Blondie and even after watching her all those years, he was amazed at how the little mare started and turned. "You just had to hold onto your left line long enough to make it past the top barrel. Blondie did the rest."

In October, at the Simcoe, Ontario, racemeet, it was father who was driving Blondie when Slim Helmle tipped out of his wagon on the barrel turn. Helmle lay unconscious on the track as his driverless outfit continued following Tom's rig. The track officials, concerned about Helmle, sent a vehicle out onto the track to check his condition. As Dorchester raced down the homestretch he saw the vehicle coming toward him. He swiftly reined his horses to the outside and turned to make sure Helmle's horses were following. Meanwhile the vehicle's driver had also swerved. Tom turned back just in time to see Blondie leap through the car's windshield.

The shattered glass severed an artery in the little mare's withers; nothing could stop her life-blood from spurting out onto the track.

"Dad just went wild when that old mare got killed," Garry remembered. "When he finally cooled down, it was one sad day around our barn, I'll tell you."

Two years after Blondie's death, Dorchester with a new lead team and a new wagon finally won a Cowboys' Protective Association, the professional circuit, championship. But he had yet to win the big one. "I can beat them all outside Calgary, " Dorchester complained, "But I just can't buy a win at the Stampede."

His racing style was a big part of his problem. Outriders couldn't catch his front-running outfit. Every year tardy outriders gave him a second here and two seconds there, and these penalties ate away any chance Dorchester had. His jaundiced opinion of outriders made him prefer to run at small shows which didn't require them, and, as his daughter-in-law Dauna recalled, "Tom never did pay much attention to outriding horses."

Young Garry had watched his father's driving techniques closely. He assembled one of the hardest running, most consistent teams in the business. He differed from his father in the belief that "You've got to have as good outriding horses as wagon horses." Garry often spent $10 to $15 a night renting proven outriding horses.

Garry Dorchester and author Doug Nelson hit the track side by side in the
1975 Calgary Stampede finals. (Nelson Family Collection)

In 1967 Garry finished ahead of his father at the Calgary Stampede, qualifying to run in the next year's final heat against the other top wagons. He ran well through the week in 1968, and by the last night his Denham Brothers rig led Ron Glass' Williams Brothers outfit by over two seconds.

He was anxious about the last night, afraid that an outrider error could cost him the championship. A young fellow named Brian Swenson had successfully loaded Garry's stove all week, but Garry decided to hire a more experienced stove man. Swenson was crushed, and begged Garry to keep him on for the final heat, "I promise I'll get it there tonight, I promise." Garry relented.

Swenson got the job done, and Garry Dorchester won the 1968 Calgary Stampede chuckwagon championship. Joining Dorchester and Swenson on the winner's podium were Garry's younger brother Dallas, and the father and son outriding team of Orville and Ron Strandquist.

Garry had accomplished in three years what his father had been attempting for close to twenty. But Garry's win broke the Stampede jinx. In 1970 Tom Dorchester won the show for his long-time sponsor Jack Sheckter and he did it again in 1971, this time for Stewart Ranches.

In 1969, 1970 and 1971 Tom also won the Canadian Circuit championship. With Garry's 1968 win, that made four consecutive world championships for the Dorchester clan. Father and son driving, and two other sons, Dennis and Dallas holding four lines as well. Combined with daughter Joan's husband, Dave Lewis, that made five family members and eight or nine wagons running at various racemeets.

Dorchesters not only dominated the dusty tracks of summer, they also held the snowy tracks of winter. For a brief period, "chucksled" racing, a Tom Dorchester brainwave, highlighted the Wetaskiwin Winter Festival.

Wagon boxes were detached from wheeled running gear and bolted onto sleighs. The poles were raised to protect the horses' legs and chains were wrapped around one runner, to keep the sleigh from sliding too far out on the barrel turns.

Dallas Dorchester won two of the three years that "chucksled" racing was part of the Wetaskiwin Winter Carnival. (Jaspers Studios, Wetaskiwin, Orville Strandquist Collection)

Ron Glass came up from High River, Orville Strandquist from Stettler, and several local drivers entered, including Bill Thompson, Bob Baird and Gordon Stewart. Garry Dorchester couldn't hold the lines with mitts, so he drove barehanded.

Dallas remembered that "It was fun, but it was cold!" Not so cold that he couldn't excel, however. Dallas won the first competition in 1968, and again in 1969.

The chucksled races were held once more, in 1974, but ended for good with the demise of the Wetaskiwin Winter Carnival.

Through winter or summer, the whole Dorchester family turned out. Tom's wife Joy, along with raising seven children, helped with the horses. She and her horse, Banner, ponied horses in the morning and walked them cool after the races at night; she was secretary or judge for many central Alberta racemeets; and when it was time to travel she was the most accomplished night driver in the Dorchester crew. Joy said that she appreciated the peace and quiet of night driving, whether it was their old three-ton, or later the big silver stockliner that she piloted down the dark roads.

While Tom Dorchester was racing at the 1973 Morris Stampede, his wagon tipped coming off the barrels and he was run over, suffering broken vertebrae. That fall he hobbled to the podium to accept the CRCA's highest award, the C.N. Woodward trophy as Cowboy of the Year. He was sixty-two and hurting. The next year he retired and sold his outfit for $10,000 to R. J. Keen.

Retirement didn't last long. In two years he brought a brand new outfit to High River and won the first, 1976, North American Chuckwagon Championship. His younger son Dallas won High River in 1977 and 1978.

The Canadian Professional Rodeo Association formed in 1979, after disagreement severed relations between the Calgary Stampede and the CRCA professional cowboys. The Battle of the Giants was staged at High River to provide the equivalent of the Calgary races in 1980. All the Dorchesters were entered, but at the last minute Tom jumped ship, to run in Calgary as an independent.

This move caused hard feelings among CPRA drivers. He had been on the board for years, but he felt his fighting days were over. While his sons Garry and Dallas raced at High River; Tom ran at Calgary.

The tradition of family involvement passed to the next generation. Garry's wife Dauna was involved in everything from keeping the books to cleaning stalls. She even made one trip around the barrels.

Driving fresh horses at Ponoka, Garry asked Dauna for help with a practice run. She climbed into the wagon and stood behind the seat so she could reach over him to grab the lines if needed. The horses lunged forward; Dauna was thrown backward into the wagon box. Garry turned the now charging horses right around the top barrel; Dauna was flung to the left. The horses swung left onto the track; Dauna was hurled to the right. As the horses raced around the track, she crouched in the jolting wagon in a spot continually showered with track dirt from the horses' flailing hooves. "Never again," she vowed, shaking Ponoka sand out of her hair, "never again!"

Garry and Dauna retired from racing in 1980, and Tom the year after, leaving only Dallas, and Joan's husband Dave Lewis in the wagon business. Sadly, Joan died in 1982, only months before Lewis won his first Calgary Stampede trophy.

Like his father-in-law, Lewis got in trouble, this time with the World Professional Chuckwagon Association. He refused to pay its new fee, 10 percent of the $20,000 he won in the Calgary final. The association refused to let Lewis drive in WPCA sanctioned shows.

He handed the lines to his stepson Rick Fraser, who set records his first three days out, at Grand Prairie's "Stompede." Fraser accepted the Joan Lewis Memorial trophy (named after his mother) and told the crowd, "My Mom loved this sport. She grew up in it, and she raised four kids in it. She was a brave woman." A fitting tribute.

Fraser resumed his role as an outrider when Lewis was invited back to the 1983 Calgary Stampede. He outrode behind his uncle Dallas to a 1984 Calgary Stampede championship. Lewis captured Calgary again in 1988 and 1990, and the ever-smiling Tom Dorchester had good reason to be proud of his dynasty. Since his retirement, his clan had won Calgary four out of nine times, and many a trophy at the shows across western Canada.

on the move

Rodeo and chuckwagon racing circuits began in the 1920s, with shows in rural ranching communities. The Calgary Stampede became the hub of the wheel, with contestants registering for spring shows, coming to the city in July, and then spreading out again. Each town simply advertised its event, hoping to get a good turnout of contestants and audience. In the 1940s a few towns began working together to create rodeo circuits, and contestants would travel from one to the other.

Cliff Claggett was an entrepreneur who travelled an organized show under his own flag.

Son of a wealthy Melfort, Saskatchewan farmer, Claggett made his own fortune in the 1930s and 1940s in heavy equipment. But rodeo was his first love, and in the spring of 1947 he used his business profits to take a travelling exhibition of cowboys and chuckwagons around his home province.

Claggett bought a chuckwagon outfit from Ron Glass, including top leader Peanuts. He hired his childhood friend Roy Stewart as stockman to care for over 100 animals.

While Roy and his wranglers cared for the stock in Saskatoon, Claggett hired another crew to build the necessary corrals and arenas at his circuit locations – Prince Albert, Melfort, Nipawin and North Battleford. Many times, part-way through a show, a truck would be brought in to plug a gap in the page wire created by a cantankerous bull or bronc.

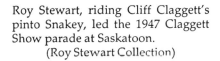

Roy Stewart, riding Cliff Claggett's pinto Snakey, led the 1947 Claggett Show parade at Saskatoon.
(Roy Stewart Collection)

Facilities were not perfect for the chuckwagons either. Iris Glass remembered a power pole standing in the middle of the Saskatoon infield. It couldn't be moved so it became the bottom number two barrel. You can bet the drivers gave that "barrel" a wide berth.

Claggett Shows began each stop on the circuit with a parade down the main street. He lured a number of top-ranked cowboys away from Alberta's spring rodeos, and wagon drivers too, including Theo Thage, Slim Fenton, Jack Lauder, Buzz Pearson, Lawson Boyd and Ron Glass.

That spring, Iris Glass and a young American trick rider, Lucy Alred, outrode behind Glass' outfit. Lucy mounted in an unorthodox fashion. Instead of swinging on, she reached her arms up and back, grasped the saddle horn behind her head and somersaulted backwards into the saddle. The crowd loved it, but Glass found it distracting. "Can't you just get on the regular way?" he often asked.

The Albertans on the crew were in for some surprises in Saskatchewan. At Foam Lake, the horses were unloaded at the stockyards and fed. The men and women went into town for their supper. When they returned, the horses were crowded into one corner of the corral. "Sweat was just pouring off them," Iris Glass explained, "and they were staring wild-eyed at their feed trough. It was crawling with cat-sized rats!" Born and raised in rat-free Alberta, Iris said, "I just went nuts. I ran over to the cab of a truck and locked myself in."

With funds short, the crew usually bedded down in trucks, tents, or in the barn with their horses. Buzz Pearson became so apprehensive about sleeping with the rats that he climbed onto a barn rafter and spent the night tied to a beam.

The spring of 1947 was cold and wet and the crowds were disappointing. Claggett the promoter was not discouraged. His barnstorming stimulated interest in chuckwagons, and brought George Stupka of Meadow Lake to Calgary in 1948 – the first Saskatchewan competitor.

In 1948, Claggett mounted an ambitious show that travelled to central Canada and the northeastern United States. It was a financial disaster, forcing Claggett to sell horses to bring the crew and equipment home.

Despite those failures, Claggett tried the eastern swing again in 1949. Roy Stewart was back in charge of the horses; his wife Jeannie cooked for the crew and also ran the midway concession.

There was no rodeo, but the performance each evening began with the entire crew riding in a grand entry. Two-year-old Reg Glass rode beside his mother, Iris. Chuckwagon races were interspersed with gymkhana events, trick riders, special demonstrations and a clown.

The show, booked to play in 27 communities, was not always a success. "I could have packed all the people on my back that came to watch us in Cadillac, Michigan," mourned Roy Stewart. In eastern Canadian towns, the chuckwagons usually ran on rock-hard, standardbred racetracks. Most had no infield and wagon races without the figure eight barrel turns weren't very exciting.

The same show that bombed in many eastern towns was a huge success back in the west, at Carman, Manitoba. Even after sharing the profits with local organizers, Claggett cleared $7,000, recouping all the losses from the rest of the tour.

To keep busy in the winter, Claggett put on indoor rodeos across western Canada. Pete Mullaney remembered a Claggett first – pony chuckwagons – miniature wagons pulled by four racing ponies.

Cliff Claggett with his white pony chuckwagon outfit in Manitoba in the 1960s.
(Faye Williamson Collection)

Claggett and his crew had to be versatile. In describing Swan River's Northwest Round-Up, Dave Theunissen wrote,

> Those who attended years ago remember Cliff Claggett singing "Saskatchewan" or "Out Behind the Barn" to fill in . . . they remember Archie Craig who wore more than one shirt each afternoon when we were short of cowboys and drove wagons at night – they remember Slim Helmle who rode bulls in the afternoon and drove chuckwagons at night as though there were no tomorrow.

In the early 1950s Cliff Claggett's funds dried up and he started a successful lumber business in northern Manitoba. He often told Pete Mullaney, "I make money to spend and to have fun – to do what I want to do." His first love was rodeo, and by the spring of 1953 he had enough money to start his travelling show again. He bought and outfitted nine trucks. To keep costs down, only the first truck was insured and licensed. When the caravan pulled into a weigh scale, the driver of the first truck presented a list of what was on all the others, and the officials let the rest drive on through. That show travelled to Sioux Falls, Ontario, then crossed into the United States.

Ron Glass, Hally Walgenbach, Tom Dorchester and Pete Mullaney were all on that 1953 trip. Their advance person was Edna Foster, who had been Claggett's secretary at his

Manitoba sawmill. Pete Mullaney remembers Foster as the best "front man" they ever had. "We never travelled looking to get rich. If [Edna] got any reception at all, she'd set it up and call to tell us there'd be a show here at such a time on such a date. We'd put it on, and lots of times we'd get enough gas money to go on down the road."

A lot of times Claggett made up the difference out of his own pocket. Eventually his pockets emptied, and the 1953 tour ground to a halt. "We were still on the U.S. side of the border," Mullaney stated. "We had no money, no food and no gas or oil for the trucks." While Claggett called home for help, his crew unloaded the horses to let them graze in the ditches. A friend wired $500 for the troupe to get home.

Pete Mullaney remembered that, "You could always tell when [Claggett] was broke because he'd disappear. Then after a couple of years he'd be back in circulation with trucks and wagons." It happened again in the early 1960s. They started out with high hopes and again the money ran out.

Along with Pete Mullaney's sons Derryl and Doyle, several other young men learned to drive chuckwagons while travelling with Cliff Claggett, including Frank Dahlgren (who rode bulls and steer wrestled in the afternoons), Bill Thompson, Gordie Bridge and Tom Glass. All four Dorchester boys, Garry, Dennis, Gordon and Dallas, travelled east with Claggett, driving either big or pony chuckwagons.

Garry Dorchester vividly recalled several excursions he made with Claggett. On one of his first trips, he was in an accident with his pony chuckwagon and came out of it with a badly broken leg.

In 1965 Garry went east with the Claggett Shows again. They'd reached Ontario when, "This guy came up and said that Cliff had left a message for us to go to Moncton, New Brunswick. Well, we only had enough money for gas . . . but we loaded up and away we went, a liner load of horses and four guys.

> "We pulled into Moncton late at night. There were no barns and it was pouring rain. We unloaded the horses. As we were tying them to the side of the liner and feeding them, this kid . . . came over. When he found out where we were from and that we figured on sleeping in the cab of the truck, he asked us to come over to his parents' place for the night."

They stayed in the family's warm, dry bunkhouse, and the boy's mother fixed them a midnight supper, and breakfast the next morning. "They sure were great people. Later on we hired the kid," Garry told me. "He rode on the ferry with us when we went over to run wagons on the [Prince Edward] Island."

They lived a rough life, sleeping in the truck, cooking eggs over a bonfire in an old car rim, but Garry said, "I don't regret it. I'd do it again."

Claggett believed in putting on a performance, and offered his drivers a bonus if they created extra excitement. Frank Dahlgren remembered a night when all three drivers in a heat decided to make some extra cash. Without knowing what the others planned, all three purposely tipped their wagons on the barrel turn.

Eldon Sergusson described wagons set up so the driver "could pull out the reach pin using a string tied to your boot. When the pin was pulled, the wagon box would drop free and the horses would run off with the pole and front wheels."

Big crowds came and enjoyed the show at Moncton, Owen Sound and Sault Ste. Marie. They took donations when their ticket-taker didn't show up, and, when challenged, they raced pony chuckwagons against stock cars – and won!

Through the late 1960s and 1970s Claggett Shows concentrated on taking chuckwagons across North America, and "pony chucks" have raced in front of sellout crowds at the Houston Astrodome every year since Cliff Claggett introduced them in 1963.

He died still a showman, practicing for a race at Morris in 1971. It was a hot July day and all but one of the pony outfits had been exercised. Claggett sent his assistants off for a cold beer while he hooked up his old experienced team by himself. Whoever had bolted the tongue to the wagon had not tightened one nut. As he started around the track, one side of the "democrat hitch" detached and the unbalanced wagon flipped over. Tangled in the lines, Claggett was dragged. The showman, who was a diabetic, had never let his illness stop him. Now the diabetes prevented the medication he was on for his injuries from working effectively, and he died a few months later, on September 17, 1971. He had planned to embark on the first ever chuckwagon tour "down under" to Australia and New Zealand at about that time.

Cliff Claggett's legacies remain. The pony chuckwagon races that he began and loved continue at Houston, controlled by his grandson-in-law, Dennis MacGillivray, and his tradition of "putting on a good show" continues everywhere that chuckwagons race.

Buddy Bensmiller went south for the winter. Fresno, California.
(Bensmiller Family Collection)

At the Cheyenne Frontier Days they have a different perspective on chuckwagons.
(The Wagner Perspective, Randall A. Wagner)

The Salmond brothers, Rene, Rod and Roger, completed Cliff Claggett's
dream by racing pony chuckwagons in Australia.
(Ed Dobbyn Collection)

12

partnership

World Champion drivers Hank Willard and Lloyd Nelson may have been partners and friends who "put on a good show" on the track, but they certainly weren't a matched pair. Willard's three hundred pounds filled a stocky five foot, eight inches, while Nelson's one hundred eighty were distributed over a lanky six foot, four.

"The summer of 1945 I was still in the air force," Nelson recalled. "I wrangled a pass to compete in the wild horse race at the Stampede, and in the evenings helped my hometown buddy Hank Willard and his brother Ole with their chuckwagon outfit.

> "Ole was driving a team with little training or racing experience; they didn't start or turn very well. Ole didn't like to lose, and about the middle of the week he asked me if I'd like to take them that night and I said 'Sure.' I must have had more nerve than brains – I'd never even ridden in a chuckwagon! I'd driven big work horses all my life, but I was scrambling for lines as the horn blew and those little running horses jumped in four different directions. Luckily the bucking chutes weren't far from the top barrel – that's what turned us that first night. But kicking the horses loose at the bottom barrel and racing around the track was the thrill of my short life! I was hooked on wagons like another fellow might be hooked on whiskey."

In 1946, Nelson was out of the air force. He and Willard decided to put together a better trained outfit.

> "We set up two barrels next to our big old barn . . . cut a figure eight around the barrels and then raced around the barn. It wasn't a very long track and it had sharp turns, but we got some training on them, especially on turning the barrels, and before long they were working pretty well and were all shined up like silver dollars."

Both Lloyd Nelson and Hank Willard learned to handle the lines working with heavy draft horses.
(Nelson Family Collection)

After a warmup at an invitational meet in Cardston, the Willard & Nelson outfit moved to Calgary.

"Our outriding crew did a dandy job at the 1946 Stampede, with three Gooch boys – Bob, Phil and Harry – riding for us, along with Windy Hellevang. They weren't experienced outriders, but all four had ridden racehorses on the bush tracks. They ran the whole week without giving us any penalties.

"Our outfit ended up third in Calgary that year. I figure that was pretty darned good for a bunch of greenhorns. By finishing among the top four wagons in 1946, Hank and I qualified to run against the top outfits in the final heat at the 1947 Calgary Stampede. From that year on we were always hooked tough."

In 1949, with Speargrass and Rambler on wheel and Chief and Tommy on lead, Willard &

The first Willard and Nelson outfit shining like new silver dollars.
(Nelson Family Collection)

Nelson finished in the top three in all but one race, and took the first CPA Chuckwagon Circuit championship. They did well again in 1950 until an accident in the mud due to another driver's interference resulted in the death of Chief and Tommy. Chief had been Nelson's favorite, his own riding horse as well as his wagon leader. "The next year," Nelson said sadly, "I stayed home and Hank took over the lines."

Willard had been content to let Nelson do the skinning, but had not wasted his time on the sidelines. He watched and learned, and as a result piloted the Willard & Nelson outfit to victory at the 1951 Stampede.

With his bulky frame and thick glasses, Willard may not have looked the part, but he was a master tactician. Ward Willard remembered his uncle calculating the effect that one extra pound had on a horse's running time. He charted the number of feet further a wagon would travel around the track for every inch the wagon ran away from the inside rail and knew precisely the advantage of the rail position. He mapped out on paper a unique wide sweeping figure eight that would have the horses running flat out when they hit the track.

"Henry made that running loop and when his horses went by the bottom barrel they were going wide open," veteran driver Phil Pollock explained. "They had their heads down and were going like Digger O'Dell. But the tracks were a lot rougher in those days and once in a while a tire would hit a stone or dig in. When you came as fast as Henry did off the long barrel, and when there wasn't much slide, he sometimes went over."

Occasionally he swung off that barrel so wide that his wagon would skid halfway across the track. But only rarely were the other outfits on the track as quickly as Hank.

A two-boy team: Ralph, Doug and Ted Nelson.
(Nelson Family Collection)

His planning continued off the track too. He toured all the other wagon barns, knew every horse, how they worked, their condition. This knowledge served him well. In 1951 he purchased a half-standardbred chestnut gelding named Skeeter from Hally Walgenbach. Skeeter was a superb athlete, who ran well in cart, relay and other races as well as on the chuckwagon. But one of Skeeter's legs had been badly gashed in an accident. At a time when good horses went for one hundred to two hundred dollars, Skeeter changed owners for five hundred dollars.

By the 1952 season Willard, with Skeeter in racing trim, had taken on a sponsor, Commodore Allen of Vulcan, Alberta. Willard and Skeeter carried the Allen tarp to another Calgary Stampede championship.

Willard's outfits seldom broke records. They won by running penalty-free, consistently. He controlled top notch outriding horses, and hired the best riders for them, men like Orville Strandquist, Bob Gooch, Norm Haynes, and Ken Buxton. He generally had two good stove men behind him, partly for insurance in case one got hurt, but also to keep one man unavailable to the competition.

Once he found a winning combination, Willard didn't change, just worked to make it smoother. Before and after the racing season he drove his teams many miles. He often travelled down a dirt road that led to Wendel and Martha Eresman's place, had coffee, then drove back. His best outfits walked in step like marching soldiers, and he believed that if they didn't step well together they wouldn't turn or run together either.

Not only did he have good running horses, but Willard, big as he was, could run a little himself. To pass the time between races, or in the evening afterward, chuckwagon men and women often held impromptu match races for both horses and humans. Bill Hamilton watched Willard win many of them. "He ran barefoot or in stocking feet, right out on the gravel in front of the barns. He could go like a steam engine. We all bet on Hank when he was running."

In 1953 Hank bought a top left hand leader named Vino Tinto. Lloyd Nelson remembered the horse as a goofball who often kicked and had a very hard mouth. But great left-hand leaders are often cantankerous and difficult to handle and Willard knew Vino Tinto's potential. He controlled the animal with a cavesson around his nose to keep his mouth closed.

Lloyd Nelson seldom travelled the full chuckwagon circuit, preferring to care for his ranching business.
Nelson and Earl cattle drive crosses the historic Bar U ranch in the 1960s.
(Nelson Family Collection)

Vino Tinto's partner Skeeter turned perfectly on the top barrel and stretched his driver's right arm to the limit when he raced around the bottom barrel. To help Vino Tinto stay with Skeeter on the barrels, Willard tied his halter shank to a ring on Skeeter's hame, so that when Skeeter turned Vino Tinto couldn't be farther than a shank's length behind him.

Hank Willard's leaders, Skeeter and Vino Tinto, pose proudly for the post-race victory photograph.
(Willard Family Collection)

In 1953 and 1954 Vino Tinto and Skeeter led Willard's outfit to two more Calgary Stampede victories, and won the coveted Charlie Beil bronze for Willard and Commodore Allen. When Willard won again in 1955, with his own name on the canvas, he became the first and only driver ever to win five consecutive Calgary Stampede titles.

During that five year period, along with the usual saddles, Biltmore hats and buckles, Willard won a number of unusual trophies. These included a chuckwagon with standard running gear, complete with box, bows and tarp, donated by Merv Dutton and Reg Jennings.

For many years Peter Hume presented a Beatty Stainless electric washing machine to Calgary Stampede winners. Willard, a confirmed bachelor, won four washing machines plus a mangle iron which his sister-in-law Edith Willard was still using in 1992.

Willard's string of victories ended in tragedy, however, not on the track, but on the road.

Shortly after the 1955 Calgary Stampede, Ernie Payne was driving Willard's truck between Hanna and Carbon. It had rained heavily, and at a tight corner before a bridge, the right front wheel caught the soft shoulder and the truck tipped over into the ditch. Skeeter was killed instantly, Vino Tinto died several days later.

Wagon drivers develop a special relationship with their animals, and the loss devastated Willard. But, as Phil Pollock stressed, "Hank only had one style . . . a terrible determination to win." The next spring Willard purchased a new lead team from Hally Walgenbach.

Willard was not the only one buying new horses in 1956. Lloyd Nelson paid Wendel and Roy Eresman one thousand dollars for a left-hand leader named Eugene D., "He turned out to be a perfect match for my right-hand leader O'Sarahan (Duke). On wheel I had a big strong horse named Icebound, hooked beside a small but mighty thoroughbred named Fox. Sometimes an outfit just clicks, and those four clicked."

After the first few nights at the 1956 Stampede, Nelson was leading, but finished the Wednesday evening with seven seconds in outrider penalties.

A cloudburst on Thursday left the track deep in mud.

> "Back then Calgary still ran six or seven flat races during the day. That afternoon the race horses had packed a narrow trail along the inside. My outfit made a good turn . . . and we got the inside position. Eugene was a real rail runner. He skinned the rail so close that Duke could run on the packed ground too. We beat every other outfit by 3½ seconds that night – made up for half the penalties in one run! We went on to win the show, by a pretty narrow margin, but we did it."

> "The day after we won, I was riding Icebound and leading the other three for their morning walk. One of the wagon men walked past, stopped, looked at me kind of funny and asked why I wasn't out celebrating. I said I was celebrating, with the guys that won me the show. Boy, was I proud of that bunch."

The first of three wins that allowed Hank Willard to take home the bronze. Mud-splattered Ken Buxton, Orville Strandquist, Willard, Bob Gooch, and Norm Haynes display their trophies. (Haynes Family Collection)

the dark side

When wagon people look back, they see not only the thrill of racing and the pride of winning, but they also see the danger. Tighter rules and revised wagon designs made the races safer over the years, but so many horses and vehicles, on so many track conditions, with so many split-second decisions to make, mean that as with any sport, something can go wrong.

The first human casualty occurred in 1948 and the victim was a spectator rather than a competitor. Immediately after the race in which his brother John won the Calgary Stampede championship, an excited Eddy Swain ran out onto the track and was hit by a late outriding horse.

Twelve years later death struck a double blow.

In 1960 Don "Scotty" Chapin contracted to drive Wendel and Roy Eresman's outfit at Calgary. On Friday, July 15, he was in 16th place. He would have to make a fast turn to hold the rail and ensure a spot in Saturday's 16-wagon final. Horrified spectators saw the wagon turn off the barrel and start to tip. Chapin scrambled to stay on top of the twisting wagon, but he failed, and was struck by the box and stove rack and dragged some distance. Rushed to the Holy Cross Hospital, Chapin died that night, leaving his widow, Buddy, and seven young children.

Less than two weeks later, death struck again.

Hitting unforgiving steel drums or wooden barrels caused many a wagon upset.
(Cosgrave Family Collection)

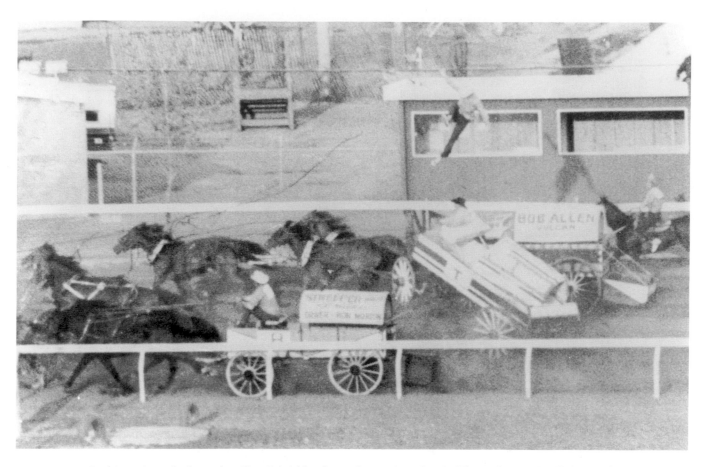

In this grainy telephoto shot, Ron David has been thrown into the air. The early evening light caught his shadow on the racehorse barn behind. (David Family Collection)

The results of stress on an old and decrepit axle. (Glenbow Archives NB-(H)-16-260)

Thirty-three-year-old Rod Bullock was one of the rising stars of the circuit. At Cheyenne's Frontier Days Bullock led a protest against the race committee's decision to run four wagons to a heat, instead of three. Cheyenne's sun-baked dirt caused wagons to slide off course as much as eight or nine feet in the turns, where on the Canadian tracks they normally slid no more than two or three feet. The *Denver Post* quoted driver Orville Strandquist, "Rod said this morning that a fellow ought to pack up and go home because of this arrangement . . . Under the conditions prevailing on this dusty track, four wagons is too dangerous."

The committee persisted. The drivers reluctantly agreed to run four to a heat.

Bullock was coming off the bottom of the long number four position when his front wheel hit a steel barrel. The wagon flipped over, throwing Bullock directly into the path of Jack Lauder's outfit, and Bullock died of massive head injuries.

The Cheyenne committee returned to a three-wagon format.

For a number of years after these two accidents, chuckwagons were advertised in the United States as "death wagons" or "coffins on wheels."

Two years in a row Lloyd Nelson's wagon tipped while turning off the long barrel. (Nelson Family Collection)

In 1971 the death toll was three.

The first occurred on Wednesday, July 14, at Calgary. Eighteen-year-old Rod Glass was outriding behind his father Ron's A.A. Bishop outfit – racing along the rail around the first turn – when a wagon clipped and knocked down his horse. Man and horse got right back up, but as Rod attempted to remount, another horse and rider collided with them. Both animals rolled over Rod, crushing him.

The grief-stricken Glass family pulled themselves together and carried on with their duties. Tom Glass, quoted in a later article in *Alberta Report*, stated "The day my brother died . . .

was the worst day of my life. But I was out riding the next night. [Rod] would have been disappointed if we did anything else."

One year earlier, 29-year-old Gordie Bridge and I were both rookies driving in the same heat at the Calgary Stampede. Gordie's wagon tipped into mine and Gordie grabbed the back of my wagon and rolled into the stove rack. He was not so fortunate in 1971. On August 2nd, he died of injuries received when he was run over by another wagon at Cheyenne.

The third fatality of 1971 occurred in September. Chuckwagon racing lost one of its most enthusiastic supporters when promoter Cliff Claggett succumbed to injuries he sustained while practicing for his pony chuckwagon races at Morris, Manitoba.

Several drivers and outriders, including Orville Strandquist and Roy David, survived potentially fatal accidents because they wore protective helmets. Another near-fatality was Ron David's "flight" of 1974.

In an effort to bring rodeo action closer to the grandstand, the British-based designers of the new Calgary Stampede racetrack had made the infield smaller, and to facilitate turning barrels inside this cramped space the settings were drastically changed.

Ron David squeezed his outfit into position on the shortest-coupled number four barrel. When the klaxon blew his horses jumped forward and he immediately cramped them on a tight right turn. The strain was too much for the wooden wagon tongue. It snapped.

"The pole went off like a shotgun," said David. "I had lots of speed built up already, and the wagon was whipping so hard I had to kneel down in the front . . . There was no possible way I could stop the horses. About three feet of pole was left sticking out the front of the wagon. Finally, around the backstretch, a wheel horse stepped on the stub and drove it into the ground."

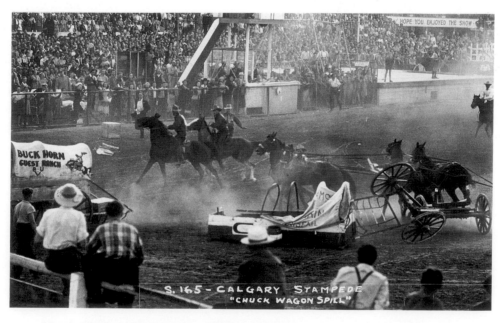

Marvin Flett's outfit escapes a collision with Johnny Swain's disintegrating rig.
(Cosgrave Family Collection)

Ward Willard, running his very first race at Calgary, had his Bob Allen outfit right beside David's. "When that pole dug in, it made the god-damnedest noise you ever heard. The pole and bolster came right up through the bottom of the box, and drove Ronnie . . . fired him up, up. I was right beside him. I looked up, and when they said Ronnie went up thirty feet, I'll bet anything he went higher."

David continued the description, from his bird's eye view.

> I hung onto the lines as I was going up until there weren't any more lines to hang onto, and I kept going. I was kind of spinning, round and round, but I can remember the track going away from me, and I remember the track coming back again, right up until I hit."

> The next thing I remember was waking up in the ambulance. Barb was there with me and my chest was puffed up about six inches higher than it should have been. The ambulance was headed down a street the wrong way – I can remember that. The driver said it was the only way they were going to get me to the hospital soon enough.

Ron remembered regaining consciousness again in the emergency room, where, "They were punching holes in me all over."

The catastrophic wreck that almost ended chuckwagon racing.
(The Calgary Herald)

He was lucky to be alive, with injuries that included fractures of six ribs, his shoulder, pelvis and back, and a punctured lung, kidney and spleen, but within a month David had a metal brace strapped to his back and was judging the chuckwagon races at Lethbridge's Whoop Up Days. He drove again the next year, and both he and Ward Willard had new unbreakable metal poles mounted on their wagons.

Yet another fatality occurred at the 1986 Cheyenne Frontier Days. Twenty-eight-year-old Edmonton native, Randy Evans, lost his life after his horse fell and he was thrown into the path of an oncoming wagon.

The spectre of sudden death rides alongside anyone who competes in a dangerous sport, be it downhill skiing or chuckwagon racing. Drivers and outriders realize the chances they take, but critics claim that unsuspecting horses should not be exposed to similar danger.

Randy Evans' death was almost completely obscured by a tragedy that occurred earlier that summer, at the Calgary Stampede. Several men were injured (Randy Evans suffered a dislocated hand) in a gruesomely spectacular crash that resulted in three horses having to be destroyed. The horses' deaths caused an understandable furore, with hundreds of letters to editors calling for the end of chuckwagon racing.

The attacks not only targeted the competitors, they included the spectators as well. In the July 12 *Edmonton Journal*, Marc Horton defined a chuckwagon fan as someone, "having a strong stomach, thick skin, no idea of fair play and an indifference to the suffering of animals."

Not all called for an end to the sport. The *Alberta Report* quoted Randy Evans' grieving mother who argued, "I'd hate to see the racing stopped. For people involved in the races, it's their whole life, just like it was for Randy." (Alberta Report, July 7, 1986).

In his diatribe, Horton railed against the "pointless exploitation of animals," and accused racers of covering up the fate of animals that are put down after the show, "because of bowed tendons and cracked bones."

What Horton didn't know, or failed to mention, was that most chuckwagon horses were saved from certain death.

Since the 1940s and 1950s, most chuckwagon racing horses have been thoroughbreds discarded because they were: too old (they were over the 10-year limit and could no longer run on approved tracks); too slow; or too difficult to handle in the tight confines of the starting gate. But most were cast off because of leg injuries.

Thoroughbreds start training on the racetrack at younger than two years of age. The stress of carrying weight often proves too much for still-growing limbs. Impatient owners or trainers cannot wait for their charges to recover and the young cripples are either shipped to an abattoir (slaughterhouse) or, in western Canada, sold as chuckwagon prospects.

Horses with severe front leg injuries cannot be ridden, but they can often be safely run in harness because the burden is pulled rather than carried.

Bonnyville's George Normand told of finding a young black gelding standing forlornly outside a meat-packing plant. "He turned out to be a three-year-old maiden [non-winner] with bowed tendons. The guy who owned him also owned the plant. I . . . bought the horse right out of the pens." At the time of the interview George had been driving the healthy horse for 10 years. (John Down, Calgary Sun, July 7, 1990).

Buddy Bensmiller, who at one time had a stable made up of 20 horses who had been destined for "the can," stated that they "just need a little time to mend and some TLC."

Grande Prairie winner Kelly Sutherland takes a business approach. "I diligently care for them. Without horsepower, after all, chuckwagon racing would be nothing."

Some detractors still believe a horse would be better off dead than consigned to a dangerous position on a chuckwagon outfit. The fact that the 1986 accident was so newsworthy proves such incidents not the rule, but an unfortunate anomaly – like a plane crash where hundreds die in one tragedy, despite the fact that air travel is statistically safer than any other form of transportation.

The number of older horses who raced or still race on chuckwagon outfits tends to show that wagon racing is not a debilitating sport that systematically uses, abuses and discards animals.

I remember my father buying a number of feisty old campaigners, Redgra, Bill's Chop Chop, Gimbo, who made good money as racehorses until "retirement" age and would have gone to the abattoir. No one could say those fellows had a terrible life. They spent seven months of the year running out on grass, free as the birds. Just after the new year they were brought into a large airy barn, comfortably stalled, well fed and exercised. And until the end of their days they were allowed to do what a thoroughbred is bred and loves to do – they raced.

Sox was a big chestnut gelding that my father, Lloyd Nelson, raised, a mainstay as either wheeler or leader from the 1950s until the 1970s. After the practice turn, Sox meant business. He bowed his neck, took the bit in his mouth and bulled single mindedly around the barrels. Sox was also a fine instructor, driven on the cart with all our new horses. If a newcomer got unruly, Sox would nip or kick it into line. When the senior Nelson retired in 1974, the senior horse was retired too.

In 1975, when I drove out of the yard for the first racemeet of the season, Sox whinnied at the truck, left the other horses and ran over to the pole fence. He ran alongside the fence as the truck rolled up the road. On his face I could see first his disgust that I had been incompetent enough to forget him, then a dawning disappointment that became disbelief and anguish when Sox realized that it was no mistake, he was truly being left behind. When he could no longer run beside the truck, Sox stood in the corner of the pasture, stretching his neck over the fence, whinnying desperately at me to stop. You can believe I had tears in my eyes as I continued up the road.

Dad said that Sox kept whinnying and running up and down the fence long after the truck was gone, and he refused to eat for days. No one who saw, or drove, Sox could say that he didn't love his occupation.

Edgar Baptiste of Cando, Saskatchewan, had a special favorite named Mr. Bushman, who for 14 years led his outfit to track records including the fastest running time at the Calgary Stampede, set in 1989 – 1:14.33. At this time the horse was a "youngster" of twenty. In 1991, Baptiste campaigned for Mr. Bushman's inclusion in the Western Heritage Centre's "Hall of Fame." That same year the horse, now a "mature" twenty-two, had led Baptiste's outfits to new track records at Wainwright and Coronation. Baptiste summed it up: "The horse just loves to race."

Bentley's Gordon Stewart doesn't believe in sending culled or old wagon horses to the abattoir. "I just can't imagine any of my horses standing around in those pens, getting beat up by other horses, waiting to die. If we have to put a horse down, we get a vet to do it."

George Normand added, "A lot of the old horses, the guys will keep them, turn them out and let them die of old age in the pasture. I just retired two this spring . . . one's 19, the other 16. Had them since they were two and four, so they're part of the family. They're going to die right out there in the pasture eating grass."

Tom Lauder owned a number of fine chuckwagon horses, but one of the finest was a big black leader named Archie. Lauder's son-in-law Jim Jensen claimed that at the start of a race Tom's leader man had to keep Archie pulled ahead with his traces absolutely tight, or the big horse would start so hard, "he would snap the single tree every time."

Ten-time Calgary Stampede winner Dick Cosgrave took a liking to Archie. Eventually Cosgrave offered more than Lauder could refuse. Several successful seasons later, however, Archie was in an accident which almost tore off one of his hooves. Lauder was nearby when the track veterinarian told Cosgrave that Archie would have to be put down. Cosgrave was about to agree. Lauder intervened. "If you are just going to kill him, Dick, give him back to me instead."

Drawing upon all the skills he had learned from his veterinarian father, Lauder soaked the hoof in a healing mixture that included sweet nitre and pine tar. Archie was normally a stand-offish horse, but Kaye Jensen remembers that Archie willingly approached the corral gate to receive his treatments. Within a year, Archie was in racing form again, and not long afterward, Cosgrave bought him from Lauder a second time.

Archie's brushes with death continued – he survived the disastrous 1942 fire at the Cosgrave barn and lived to a ripe old age. Although he no longer raced, the veteran lead horse helped young Bob Cosgrave train new wagon horses. Like the chuckwagon races themselves, the old black leader was a survivor, and the dark side of the sport most often has a happy ending.

Kay Lauder on Archie, the Survivior.
(Kaye Jensen Collection)

training

Happy endings are the result of hard work, intensive preparation and training. They may also begin with good horse stock.

Born and bred to race!
(Targhee Photo by Gordon Biblow)

Ron Glass' Casey and Peanuts were both sired by a thoroughbred stallion named Flag. Bred to grade mares, Flag's progeny proved to be outstanding chuckwagon horses, including Glass' unbeatable half-miler, Flame; Jack Gill's bald-faced leader, Headlight; Rod Bullock's wheeler, Tex; and Bill Greenwood's lead mare, Flag. Another mare, Judy Kaye, foaled Lloyd Nelson's favorite chestnut leader, Sox.

In a process similar to that of training any athlete, or any racehorse, chuckwagon drivers develop their horses' muscles and stamina in a regular spring exercise regime that usually involves driving a wagon, or ponying the animals for longer and longer periods around a cultivated field or track.

But what makes chuckwagon racing different, and so much more exciting, is the start, with its turn around the barrels. Getting horses in running condition is one thing; teaching them to start and turn is another.

There are as many methods for training top turning outfits as there are top drivers. Until 1948, drivers could use a long lash buggy whip to encourage their lead teams. An extra man was allowed on the wagon to handle this task, but most drivers transferred four lines to one hand and wielded the whip themselves.

Drivers such as Slim Swain, Jack Higgins and Slim Fenton "popped" the whip over their horses' backs or tickled their bellies with it. If Lloyd Nelson's lead team Duke and Eugene

D began to lag a little, the morning of a race Nelson would hook them on a California cart and do a few turns on the barrels, tapping them several times as they rounded the bottom barrel into the first turn.

A car horn "klaxon" sounds and Marvin Flett's horses crouch to start. Like his brother Dale Flett, and brother-in-law Dick Cosgrave, Marvin left nothing to chance, going so far as to drill with a full crew. (Cosgrave Collection)

When Orville Strandquist saw Nelson out on the track early in the morning, "I knew darned well who was going to win day money that night."

Less ambitious horses needed the reminder to run and turn, and when the whip was banned, they were no longer useful on a chuckwagon. Without a whip the leaders, the most important element in the turns, are out of reach of the driver.

Some drivers carried a pocketful of small stones that they, or someone else with a good eye and a trained throwing arm, tossed at the leaders as they made the cut around the barrels. At one meet Phil Pollock asked Ed Kroschell to toss a "hurry-up" stone at a sluggish leader. Kroschell stood in the infield and waited until the leaders started turning before he heaved. The rock missed the horse, struck Pollock's goggles, and knocked a lens out of his glasses. Pollock didn't try that trick again.

Dogs are always found around the wagon barns, but few are part of the training process. Tom Dorchester, however, used his blue heeler, Silver, to speed his lead team's progress around the barrels. When Dorchester was practicing, Silver would rush in and nip the leaders' heels as they swung around the top barrel, then the dog would race down and do the same as they cut onto the racetrack. Silver had to be locked up in the evenings or he would play his role during a race as well.

One spring in the early 1970s I recall a veterinarian placing our horses on a steroid regime which was perfectly legal, and which he insisted was absolutely safe. The steroids left us with a group of well-muscled geldings with a dramatically increased libido, but who ran considerably slower than they had the year before. We didn't continue the program.

There is little doubt that banned "racehorse" drugs have been used on some chuckwagon horses. Spot checks that were initiated at the Calgary Stampede in the 1980s seem to have stopped this occasional drug use, and there has never been a positive test.

Regulations also forbid the use of shock devices. Some chuckwagon drivers liked to use shock tactics borrowed from the racehorse barns to train their horses to start and turn. They ran electrical wires from a battery in the wagon box along the pole and out onto the horses' harness. During practice they shocked all the horses to make them start quickly together, or jolted an individual to make it turn faster while rounding the barrels or into the first turn. Normally, these devices were just for training. But an intelligent horse soon realized that it would not be shocked in an actual race and tended to forget the lesson. To rectify this situation, one driver attached a stock prod to the wagon box where he could kick it *on* with his foot to shock his horses during an actual chuckwagon race.

Marvin and Elmer Flett in a California cart race. These light carts were often used for chuckwagon training as well. (Johnny McNab Collection)

A replacement driver for this aforementioned driver was practicing starts and barrel turns at Lethbridge. As the practice horn blew the new driver jammed the stock prod on, but the handle didn't release properly and the horses received a continuous jolt! Instead of turning at the top barrel, the frantic animals ran straight ahead and leaped over a snow fence that cordoned off the practice barrel area. The horses kept running out into a steep-banked car racetrack in the centre of the infield. They made several circuits around this short track before the driver finally managed to retract the prod's handle.

One of the fastest turning outfits was owned by Calgary's Roy David. In 1972 he was unbeatable in the barrels. The other drivers voted his lead team the best and awarded them trophy halters. Roy claimed, however, that he "never would have turned a barrel" without his left-hand wheel horse, Pash's Pride. While his leaders slipped around the top barrel within inches of hitting it, "Pride charged hard and took the wagon past the barrel." To make sure he didn't hold Pride back, David fed the big horse a lot of extra line, and then, "hoped to God the leaders turned" or the outfit would have gone to the fence.

Winter workout. Lloyd Nelson feeding cows using three chuckwagon thoroughbreds and a Belgian draft mare. (Nelson Family Collection)

Another man with a top turning wagon team, Bill Thompson of Wetaskiwin, often didn't turn his horses on a set of barrels until their first show. Without help to hook four together, he exercised his horses in pairs. Other men with time or help constraints only hooked their outfits once or twice a week, exercising them the rest of the time by chasing them around the field, as Wendel Eresman did, or leading them with a ponying horse. "Doc" Doyle Mullaney strung his animals behind a well-padded truck.

Some industrious horses trained on their own time. George Stupka of Meadow Lake had a lead team that ran side by side in the pasture, making figure eight turns. Lloyd Nelson's wheel team of Fox and Icebound often did the same thing, perhaps training to move up to leaders.

Outriding horses have always been an integral part of the race, and Iris Glass felt that having well-trained and manageable ones was crucial. "There's no more just getting on a racehorse and going. We ride them at home a bunch, until they're broke. When we're practicing we ride or lead the outriding horses behind the wagon, right up against the back, over and over and over again, until they're used to the banging and rattling. The wagons are running now within one or two one-hundredths of each other," she continued. "On a close night a one second penalty can take you from first to twentieth."

Brian Swenson and Blaze were both rookies when they started outriding in the 1960s for Lloyd Nelson. Using posts and binder twine, Swenson constructed an alley that guided Blaze up and around a 45-gallon drum as the top barrel. One of the Nelson children followed Blaze with a light willow switch, as Swenson practiced leading and jumping onto Blaze again and again until they both worked perfectly. The practice paid off. In the six years he held Nelson's leaders for him, Swenson, aboard Blaze, never caused a single second of penalty.

Three outriding horses await their turn behind the Glass practice wagon. (Dale Flett Collection)

Controlling four strong and eager thoroughbreds takes a driver who is in shape for the race. When I drove it happened that I was also milking cows, so my hands and wrists were strong. But most drivers get in shape by driving. To learn to turn barrels, they turn barrels.

The barrel positions and track lengths have changed over the years. Experimentation in the first few years resulted in some strange formations, but an arrangement was agreed upon that lasted into the 1970s, when most of the smaller shows like High River copied the "softer" [easier] barrel setup adopted by the Calgary Stampede in 1974.

That easier setup has made the barrel turns much less dramatic and dangerous. A few drivers regret the change and feel that much of the thrill of the race is gone. But Richard Cosgrave believes that drivers must practice using whatever format will be used for the race. "A couple of years ago the northern guys were beating our asses to the first corner because they were running the easy barrels on their whole circuit. What's the use of us turning hard barrels all spring and then go to Calgary where they're soft?"

There has never been a school for training chuckwagon drivers. Rather than starting from scratch, most hopeful drivers, or "wanna bees," complete informal apprenticeships with veteran drivers before going out on their own.

Most outriders learn their trade on the job as well, but during the 1980s there were so few young men starting that Tom Glass and Dallas Dorchester both ran outriding schools. The schools were only moderately successful. Newcomers still found themselves in the position of needing to prove themselves under fire, to get real race experience, before anyone would hire them.

The only way to learn to drive is to drive. Lethbridge fireman Larry Mead throws the lines at them during his hometown's Whoop-Up Days.
(Larry Mead Collection)

Many young men first became interested in chuckwagon racing by working around the barns, cleaning and bedding stalls or walking and exercising horses. Usually this dirty work is done by the drivers' family or friends, so again it is difficult for "outsiders" to break into the chuckwagon world.

The chuckwagon racing world is basically a family affair, where well-trained animals, riders and drivers work all year for a few seconds cutting a figure eight and racing around a track. More time spent training ensures that less time is taken during the race – and there, less is certainly better.

Starting young – Joe King steers the leaders while son Rio grips the wheel lines.
(Targhee Photo by Gordon Biblow)

The official rodeo rule book
for 1957.
(Nelson Family Collection)

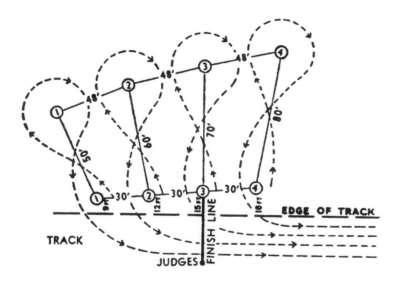

This barrel set-up was used from the 1920s to 1960.
(Nelson Family Collection)

The official Canadian rodeo rule book for 1962. (Nelson Family Collection)

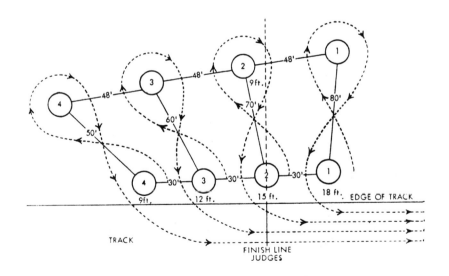

This barrel set-up was used from the 1961 to 1973. Note the numbering is now 4,3,2,1 from left to right. (Nelson Family Collection)

The 1992 Calgary Exhibition and Stampede rule book for chuckwagons. (Nelson Family Collection)

Dale Flett (centre) has plenty of help hooking up at High River in the 1950s.
(Dale Flett Collection)

royalty

R oyalty is determined not only by lineage, but by the recognition one gets within one's country or around the world.

Fifty years as a chuckwagon driver and half a century of careening around racetracks behind four high-spirited horses certainly earns Orville Strandquist a position in the regal circles of chuckwagon racing. Seventy-one year old Strandquist reached the half-century milestone when he competed at the 1991 Calgary Stampede.

Orville Strandquist loves a parade, and a prank. (Strandquist Family Collection)

Although he never did pilot a Stampede-winning outfit, Orville stepped onto the winners' podium thirteen times as an outrider, five times in a row in the 1950s behind Hank Willard, and twice later in his career in a father-and-son outriding combination with his oldest son Ron.

Strandquist was involved in many rodeo events over the years; he entered his first Calgary Stampede back in 1939 as a bull rider; for years he competed successfully in the standing Roman races and the wild cow milking competition; and he competed in steer-decorating, steer-wrestling and the wild horse race.

In 1985, the diminutive Strandquist received the prestigious Guy Weadick Award, presented each year at the Calgary Stampede to a cowboy who has diligently and effectively promoted the sport of rodeo. And in 1992, the Stampede created the Orville Strandquist award for the outstanding rookie driver of the year, as a special recognition of the old-timer's contribution to the novices of chuckwagon racing throughout his career.

A tough and feisty competitor, Strandquist was a good friend; and when he needed help, he got it as readily as he gave it.

After Orville captured the title at the 1953 Edmonton racemeet, the headline read: *The Quiet Little Bread Man Wins.* Judy Melville claimed, however, that her delivery man father was only quiet "when somebody stuck a microphone in his face."
(Glass Family Collection)

One of the family's worst moments occurred the evening of May 20, 1966, when Orville and his wife Doris lost almost everything in a fire. The flames consumed their outbuildings, their truck and gas tanks, tack, wagons, and most devastating of all, their barnfull of horses.

Looking back at the disaster, Strandquist mused, "It could have been a lot worse. If it had happened in the daytime the kids could have been in the barn playing. We could've lost one of them."

Neighbors rallied around the stricken family. The first Sunday after the fire, the Stettler community organized a benefit rodeo. More money was raised that day than at any rodeo Stettler ever held. The cowboys even donated their prize money. Communities from as far as Lake McGregor, about 400 km (250 miles) away, put on benefit dances and donated the proceeds to the Strandquists. Their neighbors held an old-fashioned bee to build them a new barn.

Orville Strandquist takes a photo break. (Strandquist Family Collection)

Because of friends and neighbors, "Financially we were probably as good as before the fire," Strandquist said in amazement. But with the chuckwagon racing season beginning, and with the Calgary Stampede only a month away, he had no horses.

A neighbor, Don Jones, offered the use of a small thoroughbred gelding named Lobo. Lloyd Nelson sent three animals up from High River: two wheelers (Sox and Moonweed) and an outriding horse, Blaze. Wendel Eresman of Arrowood donated a top racehorse named Breathless Bud, along with four outriding horses.

Strandquist had enough horse bodies to make an outfit, but the four wagon horses had never worked together before. "The first time he hooked them up," Doris Strandquist chuckled, "it looked like you'd turned chickens out of a coop."

Although the first drive didn't go well, Orville felt that Nelson's wheeler, Sox, had potential as a right leader. "The next morning I got up at four o'clock," he explained. "I told Doris to keep the kids in the house and I went out to teach Sox his name."

He hooked Sox and another horse on a California cart. Each time he called "Sox!" Strandquist snapped the big chestnut with a buggy whip. It only took a couple of snaps before Sox was responding well. That night he hooked a four-horse outfit again. He put Sox on the right-hand lead position and Lobo on the left. "I put the little sorrel up there almost as a joke, but it was no joke."

Although mismatched in size, the lead team worked well together. After only a few minutes, when Sox turned, Lobo stayed right with him.

"He had to," grinned Strandquist. "Sox came around so hard to the right he'd almost jerk Lobo off his feet; and when Sox turned left, the poor little guy had to scramble to keep from getting run over. Lobo looked like a colt, running along with his head tight against Sox."

When he came back from driving that night, Strandquist was smiling. Doris asked how the horses had worked and he said, "Oh Doris, they're one hell of an outfit!"

The new team needed to be good. They had big horseshoes to fill. The year before, the Strandquist outfit finished third at Calgary. That meant he was entitled to run in the final heat against the best outfits – the 1965 winner Bill Greenwood, and top contenders Hally Walgenbach and Ron Glass.

Because of the circumstances, some suggested that Strandquist didn't belong in that final heat. "They laughed at me. They said, 'You shouldn't be in there. You'll be so far behind it won't be a race.' "

But Orville insisted on running. "I might be behind," he told the skeptics, "but I'll have all my outriders."

The first night out, he turned alongside Greenwood and Glass, ahead of Walgenbach. "I ran three wide all the way around the track, and when I started to go past them down the homestretch I could hardly believe it. I was so excited, why, if I could've crawled out on the double trees, I would've!"

When Strandquist drove back to the barns after the race, Lloyd Nelson was waiting and smiling. Sox and Moonweed had done the job. Don Jones came up and raved about little Lobo. Wendel Eresman hurried over too, enthusing about Breathless Bud. They all had a stake in the race and they were all delighted at the result.

Strandquist's makeshift outfit finished fifth at Calgary, then travelled down to race in Cheyenne, Wyoming.

On his way back from Cheyenne, Orville stopped at High River to return the three Nelson horses. When he asked what he owed, Lloyd Nelson questioned, "Did the horses do you any good?"

"Well, I guess so! Look what they did in Calgary, and I got second in Cheyenne."

"That's all I wanted to know," Nelson replied. He wouldn't take any payment for the use of his horses.

Orville next drove to Arrowood to return the Eresman animals. They unloaded the outriding horses, but Eresman insisted that Breathless Bud stay on the truck. Strandquist protested, but was told, "No Orville, I chust gave him to you."

Many a time Orville drove the Buffalo wagon during the Cheyenne Frontier Days morning parade. (Strandquist Family Collection)

The Strandquists endured another tragedy in 1979 when their youngest son Rocky, a successful young jockey, was confined to a wheelchair following a horse-racing accident. Just the year before Rocky had filled in as a last minute replacement outrider at the High River wagon races. Rocky completed that first, and last, outriding task successfully. With the positive outlook that he inherited from his parents, Rocky now claims to be the only outrider to have ended his career without causing a single second's penalty.

Lloyd Nelson, with "Sox" on right lead, hits the track just behind Orville Strandquist's outfit.
(Nelson Family Collection)

Several years earlier Orville had vowed, "I've run against Dick [Cosgrave], I've run against Bob and Richard. Now Richard has two boys, Colt and Chad. I'll run against the fourth generation of Cosgraves before I quit.

When asked whether he thought Orville could accomplish that feat, Tom Dorchester nodded his head. "He probably will," said Tom. "The old Swede wears pretty well."

In 1992, a number of chuckwagon drivers organized a new group, the Central Professional Chuckwagon Association, to run races in a number of Alberta towns, including Stettler, Lethbridge, Medicine Hat and Red Deer. When the group invited the elder statesman of wagon royalty to join them, the seventy-two-year-old couldn't resist running just one more season.

After winning five Calgary Stampede and five World championships, Grande Prairie's Kelly Sutherland has become known as "The King" of the chuckwagon drivers. Since the age of nine, Kelly jockeyed racehorses on bush tracks and kept on until he was too heavy to ride, then started working for Dave Lewis on the wagon outfit he had in partnership with Sutherland's father.

Each spring Kelly would knock off the last couple weeks of school and catch the bus to Wainwright to work with the wagons. Neither his father or Dave Lewis was making money

With Strandquist on the outside, here come Kelly Sutherland and Chicago Mike along the rail. (Bob Morrison photo)

on the wagons, so, like the other barn bugs, he slept under the truck or in the back of the liner, and worked just for his meals.

The first year, 1966, Kelly outrode at the smaller shows, but wasn't allowed to ride in Calgary. The second year he outrode everywhere.

That second year the Sutherland and Lewis horses were stabled in the big brick barn at Calgary. One morning racehorse trainer Bobby Marsh led over a scrawny three-year-old gelding and handed the shank to Dave Lewis.

The horse's name was Chicago Mike. The evening before, Marsh had put a goat in Mike's stall, a common ploy to calm a nervous horse. When marsh came back in the morning, Chicago Mike had walked the goat to death! Tramped it right into the dust.

Lewis bought the horse and handed the shank to Kelly; payment for the year's outriding. When Kelly turned Mike loose in his new stall, the young horse circled round and round like a merry-go-round. Kelly was not impressed. "But Mike turned out to be one of the best horses I ever drove on lead," Sutherland explained. "It's those unstable,

The King, Kelly Sutherland, at the 1986 Stampede. (Bob Morrison Photo)

psychotic types that often make an exceptional leader, because they're always on edge and alert."

The spring Sutherland turned seventeen, Dave Lewis suggested he try driving. The first race he drove, at Cloverdale, British Columbia, Kelly's outfit balked. "Here I am, scared to death, never been in a race, and nothing moved! In front of a grandstand full of people all laughing because we never got off the infield."

They got back to Grande Prairie and worked the team, and got them going again.

The next week the first night at Rimbey Kelly tipped over. "That first year I upset seven times! I had an exceptional outfit, but to be quite honest, they were too much horse for me. I didn't have the ability or the strength to drive them."

He finished eighth at Calgary that year, with "a ton" of penalties, but surprised himself by winning at Morris. "I don't know how I pulled that off because I couldn't drive a wet noodle."

His second year driving, Sutherland won the nine-day show at Cheyenne and gained a lot of confidence.

> Until I won Cheyenne I was scared to drive wagons. I'd upset a dozen times and I couldn't figure out what was going wrong. Was it me? Was it the horses? Then after I started to win, I could figure it out: you only upset when you make a mistake. If you make a mistake, you pay. Once I figured that out it didn't bother me.

The youngster picked up his driving skills initially from Dave Lewis, and later from Ralph Vigen when he and Kelly travelled together. Vigen didn't talk very much, but Kelly used to ride with him and study how he turned and how he'd handle certain types of horses.

"Ralph's hands looked like two oak tree roots," Kelly explained, "but he had a special sense for communicating through the lines to his horses."

Kelly Sutherland's mentor, and five-time circuit champion, Ralph Vigen. (Bob Morrison photo)

Sutherland soon learned that winning takes more than driving skill and good horses. Just like in chess, there are psychological games played in the chuckwagons.

> People don't understand, but you get in the final heats, and there are certain guys who can dominate the situation. That's one of the biggest reasons why I've done well. Some people call it arrogance, but I know what it means to me – it's confidence. I have to display it in order for me to tick.

Kelly's patented thumbs-up victory salute is occasionally greeted by boos or even ruder gestures. But these responses don't bother him. "That's somebody else's fans, and wagon racing needs fans."

Sutherland feels that racing is a lot more competitive than when he started.

> The old guys can talk all they want about the Blondies and the good old outfits. Chicago Mike and I set track records here in Calgary and all over, but I guarantee the outfits now are going faster, they're turning quicker, and they'll do the same thing every year because we have better horses now. On average they're younger, and they're fed better; they have better vitamins, better drugs – that you're allowed to use – so naturally they're going to break records.

He hasn't pushed his son Mark into driving. "The reason I won't, or didn't, is because there would've been a big set of shoes to fill if Mark started at seventeen, and a ton of pressure. My brother Kirk lived with it for quite a while before he finally got over it."

In the early 1980s, Kelly Sutherland lost his competitive edge. He quit for a year.

The brief hiatus made him wonder about former champion Hally Walgenbach, who was still in his forties when he retired. Ralph Vigen believed that Hally was one of the best wagonmen ever – he could drive anything. When Sutherland asked him why he quit, Walgenbach said, "I lost my nerve, Kelly, no guts any more." It was either quit or humiliate himself driving dud horses.

Reflecting, Sutherland mused, "I'm the high-strung, hyper type, and that's probably what will happen to me too. I'll lose my nerve. And when I do, I'll shut 'er down."

Because they had to travel far from their Grande Prairie base, the Sutherlands were one of the first to build canvas stables for the sides of their stockliner.
(Calgary Herald Collection, Glenbow Archives)

chuckwagons for breakfast

Although royalty is usually waited upon, the kings and queens of the chuckwagon world even do the cooking – at least at breakfast. What could better represent western hospitality than sizzling hot bacon and pancakes served from the back of a chuckwagon?

These breakfasts that have become standard fare at racemeets, fairs and rodeos throughout western Canada originated at the 1923 Calgary Stampede. Guy Weadick had dictated that the streets of Calgary would be reserved every morning for "saddle horses, Indian cayuses, chuck-wagons, cowboys, and cowgirls." The tradition of serving "breakfast" was a hit from the very first, when

> Jack Morton, the man who wears the brightest orange shirt yet exposed to view, galloped the CX chuckwagon down Eighth Avenue on Friday morning, he started the final performance of the "morning stampede" in a way that Calgary will never forget . . . Four plunging horses dragging behind them a complaining chuckwagon, flanked by howling cowpunchers who rode across the tracks as if such modern improvements did not exist, made the turn around Traffic Officer Dan Finlayson and pulled up with a jerk on the south side of the avenue, between Centre Street and First Street West. Out came the old cookstove and soon the pungent odor of wood smoke filled the air, to be followed shortly by the inviting aroma of sizzling hot cakes.

Driver Grant Preece carries on a 70-year tradition. (Trudy Cowan, Museum of the Highwood)

"Who wants 'em – Who's hungry?" queried the cook. They wanted them and were hungry. Spectators fought to get to the front . . . (Calgary Daily Herald, July 13, 1923, p.1).

Other crews imitated Morton's antics the next year. The media and the crowds loved it. The Herald's headline shouted, "All Calgary Given Chuck Wagon Feed On Downtown Trail" and went on to proclaim,

> If anyone missed, it was not the fault of the cowboy cooks who handed out hot flapjacks by the thousand and syrup by the bucketful . . . The Mosquito Creek outfit started off the morning celebration with a bang. The boys galloped up . . . unhooked and hitched their horses, pitched camp, staking the wagon cover out to pegs nailed in the asphalt pavement and in a minute the old camp stove was out on the pavement and going . . . The special prize of $25 for the best stunt staged by the chuck wagon crews went to the Mosquito Creek crew. The boys of this gang boosted Miss Ruth Rogers of the Western Stock

Growers Association to the box and handed her the reins. She drove the victorious outfit through the throngs that crowded around the wagon like an experienced driver . . . (Calgary Daily Herald, July 11, 1924, p. 1).

Morton's spontaneous gesture soon became standard procedure.

Today's competitors are supplied with a propane stove, sparkling clean cooking implements, jugs of batter and boxes of bacon, and are assigned spots throughout the downtown, where they are paid to cook free breakfasts for Calgarians and visitors. Although the breakfasts have become

Downtown Calgary, Stampede Week.
(Museum of the Highwood 980-6-31T)

much more organized, the tradition of western hospitality remains the same. Back in 1979, veteran NPCA driver Dick Dye commented that the Stampede breakfasts were "an integral part of chuckwagon racing," that gave "spectators a chance to get to know the drivers." (Calgary Herald, July, 1979, interview with Dick Dye by David Hatter).

This skillful cook managed to flip a pancake on the move.
(Nelson Family Collection)

On occasion, chuckwagon breakfasts have been exported.

In 1948, Calgary football fans filled 13 railway cars and headed east to cheer their "Stamps" to a Grey Cup victory in Toronto. When word of a rowdy western invasion reached the stately Royal York Hotel, officials there "took every stick of furniture off the main floor."

During the 1950s and 1960s, members of the Lord Strathcona Horse performed in tank rodeos. These contests were discontinued because of the expense, and the danger. Korea, c. 1952. (Lord Strathcona Horse Regimental Archives)

The westerners certainly did shake up the big city. Buckskin-clad native dancers, lariat-wielding cowboys, square dancing in the streets, and chuckwagon breakfasts were all featured in the week-long pre-game party. It was stampeding Calgarians who transformed the Grey Cup from a football game into an annual national celebration.

Western traditions represent home to Canadians overseas as well. No matter where they may be stationed, the four army regiments home-based in Calgary traditionally celebrate the Canada Day weekend with a Stampede parade and rodeo events. And they always kick off the celebration with a traditional chuckwagon breakfast.

The 1st Princess Patricia's Canadian Light Infantry (1PPCLI) took their celebration to Cyprus with them in 1978.

> The 1PPCLI Calgary Stampede was an enjoyable challenge for the contestants in the various events and provided a uniquely western brand of entertainment for the many guests. The Stampede breakfast started bright and early but this did not prevent the approximately 30 official guests from enjoying "home cooked" hotcakes, bacon and eggs with all ranks of 1PPCLI . . . Stampede events got underway at 08:30 hours when Drum Major Point and the 1PPCLI Corps of Drums led the Stampede Parade, which featured some original and interesting company floats . . . "B" company and HQ company tended towards the more traditional chuckwagons pulled by a donkey.

The chuckwagon participation was not limited to serving breakfast, there in faraway Cyprus. At home in Wainwright, Alberta:

> The all time favorite chuckwagon races were run individually by each 'coy' against the clock. The course consisted of a skill testing dash around several barrels, followed by a gruelling pull at breakneck speeds around the sports field. "B" company recorded the best time . . . (RIC-A-DAM-DOO, July 21, 1978, p. 3).

Mock chuckwagon races and breakfast were also used to let off steam and to maintain a connection to home by the Canadians sent to participate in Operation Desert Storm in 1992.

In the summer of 1991 a Calgary couple decided to escape the hustle and bustle of Stampede festivities. They booked two tickets to Australia for the first week in July. Weren't Bob and Sheryl surprised when they stepped off the plane to be greeted by Aussie friends dressed in western attire who immediately drove them home for a Stampede breakfast of flapjacks and fried eggs, and sausages done on the "barbie."

Donkeys were the order for this parade day in Egypt.
(Lord Strathcona Horse Regimental Archives)

Yes, the chuckwagon spirit was there, half-way around the world in Australia, as it has been in Cyprus and Kuwait, in Cheyenne or Houston, in Toronto, or back home in southern Alberta.

In December of 1988 the Calgary Cares Team travelled to Cyprus where they whipped up Stampede-style breakfasts for members of the Canadian Contingent.
(Lord Strathcona Horse Regimental Archives)

two northerners

At the 1991 Strathmore Rodeo, just inside the chuckwagon competitors' enclosure, two mobile homes sat facing one another. One belonged to Buddy Bensmiller, leading driver on the Northern Professional Chuckwagon Association (NPCA) circuit, just back from winning Cheyenne; the other to George Normand, leading driver on the World Professional Chuckwagon Association (WPCA) circuit, coming from a second place finish at Kamloops, B.C. Their trailers, corrals, stockliners and wagons sat side by side as well. Both Bensmiller and Normand make their living from chuckwagon racing, some horse training and trading, and the generous support of their sponsors – Majestic RV for Normand and Chinook Centre for Bensmiller. Despite the fact that they represent two rival organizations (NCPA and WPCA), Bensmiller and Normand remain the best of friends.

Both grew up in northeastern Alberta; Bensmiller near Dewberry, Normand near Bonnyville. They were born only months apart and have known each other since they were seven-year-olds competing in gymkhanas. At nine, they were both jockeying their fathers' racehorses on bush tracks.

Buddy's father, Allen Bensmiller, had been racing chuckwagons at local events since the 1950s and was one of the founders of the Northern Chuckwagon Association (NCA, which later became NPCA) in the early 1970s. Buddy "lived on horses" when he was a youngster. To help keep his father's animals in shape, he would ride an outriding horse to and from

Allan Bensmiller and his outfit at the 1950 Grunlawn picnic. (Bensmiller Family)

school. He was 12 when he first outrode behind his father's outfit at St. Walburg, Saskatchewan.

1959 "Trophy Winner" at the Meadow Lake Stampede. Allan Bensmiller in his chuckwagon and outrider Bruce Craige. (Bensmiller Family Collection)

George's father Maurice Normand drove chariot teams and then "got the sickness of driving four instead of two." The boy was 13 when he outrode for the first time, also at St. Walburg, behind Pat Ross' Meadow Lake rig.

Buddy and George were both busy outriding, and rarely got the chance to drive with their fathers. On the sly, George hooked up teams in the afternoons when his father was at work. "Dad wouldn't have found out except for one time I took out a chariot team and one horse started kicking . . . it's lucky he never kicked me in the head, but he busted the doubletree all to heck. I couldn't fix all that stuff before Dad came home."

When he was 16, Buddy Bensmiller came to the Calgary Stampede to outride for Dallas Dorchester. That same year Normand outrode for his father's outfit at a CRCA show (later to become WPCA) in Lethbridge. George was first of the two friends to start driving a chuckwagon. In 1976 he drove on the NCA circuit and Buddy outrode for him.

The next year Normand travelled the CRCA professional circuit long enough to qualify for a position in the 1978 Calgary Stampede. Bensmiller stayed up north and ran a wagon on the NCA circuit.

Normand did very well at the 1978 Stampede, finishing in sixth place his first time out. That winter Maurice Normand purchased an outfit for Bensmiller to drive on the southern CRCA circuit.

A youthful Buddy Bensmiller drives his chuckwagon while George Normand runs ahead after releasing his leaders. (Bensmiller Family Collection)

The friends' reunion was not to happen yet. The rupture between the representatives of professional rodeo and the Calgary Stampede Board resulted in the Stampede inviting alternative organizations to compete in 1979. Bensmiller did not have to wait a year to qualify. His NCA wagon would run at Calgary, while Normand and his professional mates organized The Battle of the Giants to run at High River.

The media quoted bitter comments from professional drivers about the inferior capability of the northern wagons. NCA spokesmen more or less ignored the accusations until the one professional driver who had left the CRCA to run at Calgary, Tom Dorchester, struck Bensmiller's outfit along the backstretch. Three horses died as a result of the crash. NCA representatives immediately condemned the cut-throat driving styles of the professionals. Comments quoted in the media from an angry Bensmiller added fuel to the fire. Bensmiller refused an offer of replacement animals from Tom Dorchester. Bensmiller's father sacrificed his own chances for a top four finish by taking the two best leaders off his own outfit and giving them to his son.

The next evening Buddy drove his father's lead team to the fastest time of the night. He continued to use his father's horses and won the Stampede's first "sudden death final," for $20,000. At 23 he was one of the youngest Calgary Stampede champions.

For two years Bensmiller ran with the NCA at Calgary while Normand continued on the professional circuit. Normand dropped out for three years to work.

In 1985 Normand bought a brand new outfit and travelled with the WPCA circuit. Amazingly, his rookie team won the circuit championship and qualified for Calgary.

George Normand was the first of the two friends to qualify for the Calgary Stampede.
(Bob Morrison photo)

But Buddy was the first to win the big show.
(Bob Morrison photo)

Finally, in 1986 the two friends ran their first race against one another. Because they competed on different circuits, Calgary was usually the only place they met. Their on-track competition peaked in a memorable contest during the final race of the 1989 Calgary Stampede for $50,000.

When the klaxon sounded, Bensmiller made a rapid turn off the number two position and went to the front. Richard Cosgrave turned quickly enough off the number one to hold the rail position, but the running was soft along the inside. Dallas Dorchester provided stiff competition from the outside, while Normand pulled in behind the other three as they ran side by side around the track. Bensmiller's team looked like they'd hold the lead, until George Normand, the Bonnyville Bullet, turned on the afterburners and came rocketing up from his trailing position. His coal black wagon whooshed past Dorchester, then Cosgrave, and was right beside Bensmiller's red wagon as they crossed the finish line. The judges went away to study the photo-finish film.

In the most exciting Stampede final ever, all four wagons finished within one second of one another, but the official photograph from the grandstand's "eye in the sky" showed that Bensmiller had managed to hold his lead and win the $50,000 by a fraction. Red beat black by only .08 of a second.

Normand wasn't overly disappointed. Off an almost-impossible barrel position his horses had put on an amazing performance.

In the 1989 dash for $50,000, all four rigs finished within a few feet of one another. Only eight one-hundredths of a second separated the two friends. (Targhee Photo by Gordon Biblow)

From 1979 through much of the 1980s, chuckwagon racing harbored a dispute between the NCPA and WPCA organizations. The animosity between the WPCA and the NPCA still lurks in a few corners, but thankfully it never darkened the friendship between two great competitors and friends, George Normand and Buddy Bensmiller.

Congratulations after the race. Buddy left and George right. (Calgary Exhibition and Stampede)

18

outriders

Buddy Bensmiller, Richard Cosgrave, and George Normand got their initiation as early as twelve or thirteen, but few as early as Gary Lauder's son Thomas. Every night during the 1991 Calgary Stampede three-year-old Thomas ferried outriding horses across the track to the infield pens.

Because they know their family's horses well, many youngsters outride for the first time behind their relatives' rigs. Some young men have enjoyed considerable success their first year of racing.

One of these was Jason Glass, who in 1987 as a sixteen-year-old rookie outrider followed his father Tom's outfit to a Calgary Stampede championship. Young Quinn Dorchester, son of Dallas and grandson of Tom Dorchester, rode his late grandfather's horse Ering to victory behind his father's outfit at the 1991 Calgary show.

Other family connections include the first father-son outriding combination of Bill and Normie Haynes, both riding for Bob Heberling's Calgary Stampede winning outfit in 1950. Orville Strandquist and his son Ron accomplished the same feat twice when they mounted the grandstand stage behind Garry and Tom Dorchester's winning outfits in 1968 and 1970.

The practice turns are over. Leader men Gary Lauder (foreground) and Jim Nevada wait for their wagons to return. (Doug Nelson, Museum of the Highwood)

Not all rookie outriders' experiences are as pleasant. In 1991, in his first ride behind Bonnyville's Ray Croteau, rookie Eddie Melville (Orville Strandquist's grandson) had the misfortune to knock down a barrel. The outfits were racing down the homestretch when Croteau's head rider noticed Eddie and shouted, "Kid, I don't ever want to see you again!" Eddie didn't go over to collect his payment for that ride.

Although a few women have outridden at smaller shows, only one woman has competed at the Calgary Stampede. May Gorst was seventeen years old in 1979 when she accompanied NCA drivers south to Calgary to replace the CRCA professionals. Gorst had been outriding since she won the rookie's outriding award for her circuit in 1976. At the 1979 Calgary show she followed Dick Dye's rig from Meadow Lake and also rode for Jim Knight of St. Walburg. She competed for several years, always insisting that she receive no special concessions, that she be treated the same as her two outriding brothers Gary and Chester.

Around the fourth turn May Gorst, the only woman to outride at Calgary, is right beside her wagon. (Bob Morrison photo)

There are many other examples where three or more family members competed in the Calgary Stampede chuckwagon races. The Swain, Flett and Gooch families all produced three or more sons who outrode or drove. During the 1970s five of Wilbur David's sons competed at Calgary: Les, Roy and Ron David drove wagons, while Butch and Larry, along with Roy and Ron, outrode.

Outriders were originally members of a ranch crew who followed their own wagon. By the late 1930s, however, the number of chuckwagons competing increased, and drivers began hiring experienced men to ride behind more than one outfit.

Dale Flett did not discourage his men from riding behind other outfits, but he did expect them to ride for him in any situation, and he paid well for this allegiance. When other drivers were paying five to ten dollars per ride, per night, Flett paid his men twenty dollars, plus another twenty per ride if he finished the week in the top four. It was seldom, in the mid-1950s to late 1960s, that Dale Flett's outfit was not among the top four wagons at Calgary.

Outriders don't have time to step into a stirrup to mount – they simply grasp the horn and swing into the saddle. Here Orval Flett is caught in mid-hop. (Haynes Family Collection)

Experienced outriders are happy to advise the rookies. One of the hazards this rookie was warned about when I first rode at Calgary were the soft spots along the old track's grandstand stage. Every night the grounds crew dug up a number of spots, several feet from the stage to set the posts for an addition to the stage for the grandstand show. The resulting "soft" spots were notorious for causing running horses to stumble and fall. Most veteran outriders rode to the outside of the track down the homestretch, but they made sure to stay a good two to three metres (six to nine feet) away from those areas, and yelled a warning if a rookie rider strayed too close to the stage.

Until the 1965 Calgary wagon races, outriders looked forward to the occasional ride in the mud. A muddy track slowed the wagons and made them easier to catch. But that year, "It rained every day and the track went past mud," Lark IsBell remembered. "It turned into a boot-top deep soup with hard pan underneath and the wagons speeded up. They were running just about as fast as on a dry track."

IsBell was following Lloyd Nelson that year. One night, the stove was safely thrown into the back of the chuckwagon. IsBell was halfway into his saddle when he became wedged between his own horse and another rider's. The two animals carried him that way around the barrels. Once they were out onto the track, however, they parted company and IsBell dropped free. The mud sucked him down, jerking his hands off the slippery saddle horn. Lark continued to cling to the lead line as his mount ran down the track. "When I finally lost the last knot on my lead line, I was surfing flat out on the deep mud."

Jason Glass following his father Tom's outfit. (Doug Nelson, Museum of the Highwood)

An outrider's saddle must be secure. Ross Nelson tightens the cinch while Kaye Jensen holds his horse. (Doug Nelson, Museum of the Highwood)

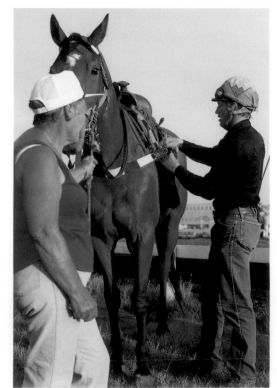

1992 was another wet year. Outrider Jim Nevada watches as Carol Alstott cleans mud off the outriding bridles. (Trudy Cowan, Museum of the Highwood)

A fine rider in almost any situation, outrider-stuntman Brent Woolsey trains a "falling" horse near Longview.

(Brent Woolsey Collection)

outriders 141

He escaped with a few bruises, but with every inch of his body coated with mud. He looked like a living statue of an outrider.

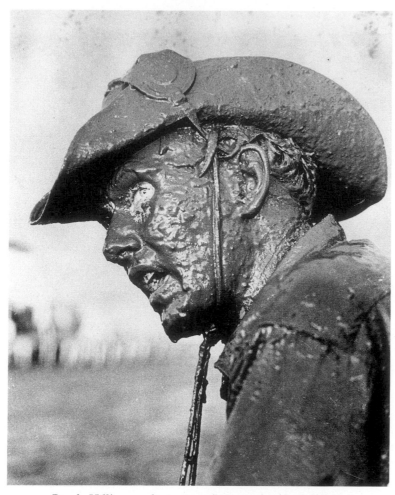
Randy Hill's award winning photograph of Lark IsBell.
(IsBell Family Collection)

The next morning someone knocked on the door of the IsBell camper, calling, "Hey Lark! You've made the front page of the newspaper." Photographer Randy Hill's award-winning image of IsBell will always be a reminder of the 1965 Calgary Stampede – the year of the mud.

Eventually an elite group of professionals took most of the outriding jobs each night and they ended up wearing eight or nine shirts at a time. For over forty years Orville Strandquist was one of the best in the business. The diminutive Strandquist joked that he "almost looked like a man" when he was wearing his full complement of shirts at the beginning of an evening of racing. All those layers could be hot on a warm evening, but on cool or damp nights outriders reluctantly stripped off the last couple of shirts.

A rider had to be careful to put on his shirts in the right order, last heat on first and so on, until he had the first heat's shirt on the outside. Drivers' wives or helpers often taped or wrote a rider's name at the back of his shirt collar, so he got the right size back from the wash. Outriders came in all sizes; from Orville Strandquist or Sammy Sisson small, to Donny Allen, Clarence Peters or Frank Dahlgren extra-large.

Those last three needed their extra size to throw 23 to 34 kg (fifty to seventy-five pound) stoves. With the light five to ten pound versions used now, the man throwing the stove is usually the weakest of the three men behind the wagon. But in earlier days the stove man was the most important. He had to be strong enough to heave the heavy "stove," yet agile enough to jump onto his horse and ride.

Another big man, Airdrie's Ron David, had the dubious honor of throwing stove behind Kelly Sutherland's great outfits from the mid-1970s.

"One year Kelly had such a hell of a starting outfit that I missed the stove three times," explained David. "He had one wheeler that rocked back and forth, and if the horse was going ahead when the horn went, there wasn't anybody could load the stove."

"After I'd missed a couple times, I told Kelly he better try somebody else, but the other two fellows missed as well. That outfit was kind of funny in that they really went ahead for about twenty feet, then dogged it a bit to the top barrel, then really charged back to the track again. I sometimes thought if I could just carry the stove up about twenty feet they'd slow enough so I could get it in, but those stoves back then were fifty pounds, and bulky; it just wouldn't have worked I guess."

The man throwing a heavy stove needed both hands to do the job, so he held his horse's lead line either under an arm (not too effective) or in his mouth. One of the best stove men of the 1960s, Lark IsBell, had to retire from outriding after his dentist fitted him for false teeth!

Next to the stove man, or perhaps equal in importance, was the leader man, the fellow who stands between the barrels and grabs and holds the leaders as they stand at the barrels. He controls when and where the horses stop and how they point toward the top barrel at the start. He also must make sure the leaders stand ahead with their tugs (traces) tight. If there is slack when the klaxon sounds and the horses lunge forward, the resulting jerk may break a tug or even a singletree.

The lead horses can make the leader man's job a lot more difficult. Roy David had a cantankerous chestnut named Robert H, who nipped and bit leader men. "That horse had Eddie Wiesner plumb terrified," Roy David recalled. "I guess Robert must have chewed on Eddie a time or two."

Robert H's reputation got so bad that David had difficulty finding men who would hold his leaders. One afternoon he asked if I would ride for him the final night at Calgary. After I agreed he started to walk away, then turned, casually mentioning that I would be holding leaders, and ran off before I could retract my agreement.

Each lead team is a little different, some quirkier than others. Bob Cosgrave had a pair of leaders that could not be held at all. They would back into the wheelers if anyone tried to grab them, so Cosgrave's leader man just stayed out of their way.

The two men throwing pegs stand on either side of the stove man, each holding one of the pegs attached to the canvas fly. The fly and pegs are each five and one-half feet long. The pegs are weighted on the end to make them throw better. These heavily weighted ends have been known to strike drivers in the back, so many wagons are fitted with a canvas deflector to protect the man on the seat.

When the starting klaxon sounds, the peg men heave their pegs into the back of the wagon. Teamwork is essential; they must throw at the same time or the fly will jerk the quickest peg back out of the wagon box.

Their individual tasks completed, the outriders must run to their top barrel and jump on their horses without bumping into one another, or the barrels. Then they must follow their wagon around the figure eight, circle the track, and finish within 38 metres (125 feet) of their wagon. Any deviation means penalties.

Four wagons rumble into the first corner. Notice that the outside driver already has all his outriders.
(Targhee Photo by Gordon Biblow)

During the 1960s and 1970s, drivers were allowed to run up to two wagons at the Calgary Stampede. Many drivers would use the same four outriding horses behind both. When the heats were drawn at the first of the week, allowances were made for at least a one or two heat rest between a driver's two races. The last night of racing, however, the rigs running in the final four heats were arranged in the order of their aggregate times. Occasionally that meant an owner-driver would have his two wagons drawn together, and he would have to hire another man to drive one of his outfits and find another four horses and outriders.

Hally Walgenbach was a popular man as well as a fine driver. Both his outfits were usually in the final sixteen at Calgary. One year in the late 1960s both wagons were drawn in the same heat, but he had little trouble borrowing enough horses and another crew.

Lark IsBell had been the regular stove man behind both Walgenbach outfits all week. In that final heat, IsBell threw the stove, mounted his horse and scooted out onto the track. In no time at all he caught Walgenbach's wagon. Although he was in the dust trailing the pack, Hally had a ready smile for Lark. As the wagon skittered around the final turn Lark took up his normal position beside Hally's leaders and shouted to urge them on down the homestretch.

When the race ended, Lark slowed his horse and returned to the infield. Imagine his surprise when Hally's wife Eleanor berated him for being late.

"It couldn't have been me," IsBell argued. "I was right alongside Hally's lead team as we went across the line."

"You were beside the wrong damned wagon," Eleanor huffed. "The one you were supposed to be riding for won the race — probably would've won day money without your one second!"

As were the days of the range roundups, the chuckwagon racing season is relatively short. Outriders must find alternate jobs to supplement their income. Jim Shield of Milo, Alberta, follows the pattern of earlier cowboys by managing a Calgary bar during the off season. Several times a runner-up for the world outrider championship, Shield won his first WPCA outrider title in 1992. He enjoys outriding and the job pays him relatively well. Shield and other top riders, Lyle Pambrun and Jim Nevada, make over one hundred dollars per ride and during a good summer can collect between $12,000 and $14,000 for three months' work.

These men earn their money. I know from experience the hard life of an outrider. During the mid-1970s I normally outrode for seven heats and drove in another. More often than not, the drive was a bit of a break.

An outrider sets his stirrups high, jockey height, to sit up off the saddle and ride his horse properly. This puts considerable strain on his knees and back. The ironic part of outriding is that the best, and fastest, outfits usually run in later heats, when an outrider is getting tired yet needs all his energy and concentration. If the track is wet there is the added difficulty of trying to jump up out of the boot-sucking mud.

There are other hazards.

A breather while the track is being harrowed.
(Targhee Photo by Gordon Biblow)

Veteran driver and outrider Orville Strandquist remembered an incident at the Stampede in the late 1940s.

"This wagon was rattling around the first turn when its tin stove bounced out onto the track and [outrider] Bob Lauder's horse stumbled over it," said Strandquist. "When the horse fell, Bob got thrown over its head and into the stove rack — the stove fell out and Bob fell in. Bob was knocked out cold. His legs dangled over the side of the stoverack all the way around the track. About the time the wagons were coming down the homestretch, Bob woke up. He came across the finish line looking just like an owl. His eyes were bulging, big and round, and his head was just a-swivelling. Even old Dick Cosgrave [then the arena director] couldn't help laughing."

Strandquist's son had his own close encounter of the chuckwagon kind.

"My outriding horse cold-jawed on me after we turned the top barrel," said Ron Strandquist. "The darned horse threw his head in the air, ran straight toward the track and crashed right into the side of Garry Dorchester's wagon."

The force of the collision tipped the chuckwagon up on two wheels and knocked driver Dorchester to his knees. Ron Strandquist was thrown out of his saddle and flew over the wagon box. "I grabbed the hoops on the way by and swung down inside the wagon."

Garry Dorchester struggled back onto his feet and finished the race, while the outrider crouched in the back of the box, "waving at the other outriders," who were clustered around and behind Dorchester's wagon.

At the end of the race Garry had trouble stopping his outfit. He had bruised his elbow when he was knocked to the floor. Strandquist could see that Dorchester was having problems, so he crawled up behind the seat. "I was going to ask Garry if he needed help pulling up," explained Strandquist. "When I tapped him on the shoulder, Garry almost jumped off his seat. He just about had a heart attack because he didn't know I was back there."

The senior Strandquist started outriding in the 1930s, when a man was lucky to make between two and five dollars a ride, and when he "fed himself . . . and went to the river to drink."

In a career that spanned six decades, Orville Strandquist was one of the best outriders of all time, winning Calgary thirteen times and acquiring seven championship buckles. After he gave one to each of his seven children, there was nothing for him to do but continue to wear his old, worn Wild Horse Race buckle.

Even with all his experience, Orville still admitted to having felt the same tension on every ride of his career. "I was just as nervous and worried the last horse I ever got on as the first time I rode, thinking 'Am I gonna make a mistake? Am I gonna do it right?'"

sponsorship

A major element of chuckwagon racing that helps wagon outfits "do it right" is the support they receive from their sponsors. Dale Flett's sponsor for most of his career was Calgary oilman Peter Bawden. "Without him, I wouldn't be here," Flett toasted. "Even if you win everything on the circuit, you just break even." (Calgary Albertan, July 13, 1963) Although Bawden's support varied with the vagaries of the oil business, his relationship with Flett produced five Calgary Stampede and four CPA titles. ·

Jean Flett poses for the victory photo in place of her injured husband, Dale. Left to right: Norm Haynes, relief driver Hally Walgenbach, Harry Schmaus, Jean Flett, Jim Lauder, sponsor Peter Bawden, and Orval Flett. (Haynes Family Collection)

Over the years chuckwagon sponsorship has assumed different forms. Of the six wagons that competed in the first races in 1923, only two – Jack Morton's and Clem Gardner's – were owned and driven by an individual rancher. The other four were pool wagons, supported by two or more ranches from a particular district. The winning Mosquito Creek

The evening sun slants past the grandstands to illuminate the Newall Bros. wagon.
(Bill Tidball photo)

Ward Willard's Ranchmans outfit proudly prances past a cluster of hot air balloons, after coming
from behind to win the 1981 Battle of the Giants. (Targhee Photo by Gordon Biblow)

Coming off barrel position number one is Wendel Eresman's green and yellow outfit – a perennial winner of the Most Colorful Chuckwagon award. Wendel was the last man to run his own canvas, Eresman Brothers, at the Calgary Stampede. (Targhee Photo by Gordon Biblow)

Roy David's Heritage Park/Co-op supporters flock to racemeets across the province, speckling the crowd with their bright yellow shirts and jackets. (Targhee Photo by Gordon Biblow)

outfit, originally piloted by the Streeter ranch's Bill "Sourdough" Sommers, was backed by the Cross, Riley, Drumheller and Macleay families.

Tom Lauder won the 1924 "show in partnership" with Ray Bagley. In 1925, winner Jim Ross' canvas carried colleague Bayse Collin's name as well. Even the great champion Dick Cosgrave accomplished his first Calgary Stampede victory in 1926 with support from Archie and "Cap" Miller.

Between 1926 and 1946, however, the majority of Stampede winners owned and drove their own outfits.

Dick Cosgrave's brother-in-law, Marvin Flett, was the first man to sell space on his wagon's tarpaulin to a sponsor, Cliff Cross' Buckhorn Ranch from Beaver Mines, Alberta. The selling of tarps caught on and other sponsors entered the chuckwagon business. In 1946 Ron Glass and Johnny Phelan were the first driver-sponsor combination to win the Stampede. The pair won again in 1947 and 1949. They were followed by Hank Willard and Commodore Allen in the early 1950s.

By 1956 when Lloyd Nelson drove his L. O. Nelson outfit to a Calgary Stampede chuckwagon championship, the days of the owner-driver had ended. Sponsors were the norm rather than the exception.

Sponsorship arrangements were and remain varied. Marvin Flett received his payment "on the hoof" from his second sponsor, Newall Brothers of Rockyford. For a year's racing, Flett received five purebred Angus heifers. After Marvin Flett retired, Newall Brothers continued a family tradition, backing Flett's nephew Bob Cosgrave and later Bob's son Richard, for a 17-year run as wagon sponsors.

Newall Brothers sponsorship was a real family affair. Some family members helped paint the attractive orange and white wagon and tarp; others sewed shirts for the competitors, and for family and friends too. After the big wagons became too expensive, the Newalls turned to sponsoring pony chuckwagons.

Most sponsors pay a set amount to have their name carried on the chuckwagon driver's canvas, but a few have a real stake in the racing outfit and even own some of the horses and equipment. Fracmaster owned its own high-tech wagon and hired Grant Profit to drive it in the early 1990s.

As well as a high-tech racing wagon, Fracmaster also made a child-size model.
(Doug Nelson, Museum of the Highwood)

Because of the variety of ownership arrangements, the division of racing spoils is mixed as well. In describing his relationship with longtime sponsor Jack Sheckter, Tom Dorchester stated succinctly, "Jack gets the trophies and the glory, I get the money."

For many drivers, a sponsor's money makes up the shortfall between purse monies and the expense of running a contending chuckwagon. In their glory years together many drivers' names become synonymous with their sponsor: Glass and Phelan, Flett and Bawden, Dorchester and Sheckter, the early Kelly Sutherland with his black and white Archie Hackwell rig, Buddy Bensmiller and Chinook Centre, George Normand and Majestic RV World, and the unique relationship developed between Totem Building Supplies and the father and son drivers Tom and Jason Glass.

Although most sponsors, like the drivers, are based in Alberta or western Canada, a few have come from farther afield. During the 1960s and 1970s, Les Cahan of Toronto sponsored Orville Strandquist. The Al Wyrick outfit from Montana supported Eddie Wiesner in the early 1970s.

From 1936 to 1974 advertising on a wagon canvas was limited to the name of an individual or ranch. In 1975 the Calgary Stampede allowed "qualified" business names to be displayed on the tarp. Sponsors received exposure with their company name proclaimed to the grandstand, and to radio and television audiences.

Wagons and canvases are a blur as they shoot into the first turn.
(Bob Morrison photo)

Opening the market to commercial advertisers pushed many individual and agricultural sponsors to the sidelines, but backers Merle Anderson and L.K. Ranches continued to sponsor their drivers. A wealthy Carbon, Alberta farmer, Anderson continued his sponsorship until he died.

Bob Morrison's award-winning photo series of Orville Strandquist's tipped chuckwagon. "If Orville had been killed or badly hurt I would have ripped the film out of the camera," said long-time friend Bob. (Bob Morrison photo)

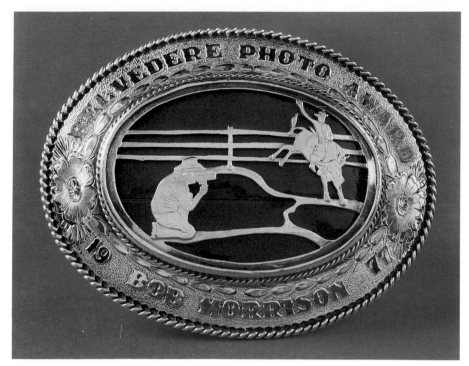

Belvedere Photo Award belt buckle, presented to Bob Morrison for his timely shots on the facing page.

Neil McKinnon's family had been involved with range chuckwagons since the 1800s and their L.K. Ranches continued to support either Joe King or Roy David through the 1970s. McKinnon felt that chuckwagon sponsorship was valuable to his feedlot and beef slaughtering operation. Cattle buyers and sellers became familiar with the company name at racemeets throughout Alberta. At shows outside the province, McKinnon found it more useful to have the wagon carry his Cedar Log Homes logo instead.

Just like drivers, some sponsors are better than others. Lloyd Nelson recalled one well-heeled backer overheard berating his driver for being beaten "by those other two-bit outfits." One of Ward Willard's early sponsors suggested he "roll the wagon and get some more media coverage for my company." I had a sponsor who borrowed a chuckwagon to use for publicity, and never returned it.

Such experiences are unfortunate because most sponsor-driver relationships are enjoyable and mutually beneficial, such as my time with sponsor Jack Curzon.

Stampede Queen Hally Strandquist smiles as the bid rises.
(Lynn Cartwright, Museum of the Highwood)

In 1978, the Bonnyville Bullet, George Normand, moved from the Northern Chuckwagon Association (NCA) to the professional CRCA circuit. The difference in sponsorship fees amazed him. "We used to run up north for $500 to $1,000 a year and really thought we were doing something," Normand remembered. "When I came south and got $5,000 from Cowley and Keith just to run in Calgary, and another $2,000 for the rest of the circuit, I figured I'd really hit the big time."

Garry Dorchester gained his most lucrative sponsor, Sikanni Oilfield Construction, in 1976, but the relationship only lasted a few years. It ended when Garry, a CRCA member, could no longer compete at Calgary. Having their company name on Dorchester's canvas had been worth $10,000 a year to Sikanni, but without the exposure at the Calgary Stampede, the company could no longer see a benefit to sponsoring Garry.

The annual Calgary Stampede "Canvas Auction" began in 1979, to gain sponsors for the little-known drivers from the NCA. Since then, the auction has proved a boon to those drivers who do not excel at marketing themselves, or who are at the lower end of the competitive scale. Many potential sponsors also enjoy the excitement of bidding for the services of the drivers. Top drivers are sponsored for figures well in excess of $50,000.

Some sponsors make their arrangements before the auction. For a three-year period from 1989 to 1991, Kelly Sutherland drove under contract to PetroCanada. Sutherland had a clause attached to the contract which specified that he be the first driver chosen at the auction.

Four wide into the first turn.
(Calgary Exhibition and Stampede)

Detractors of the tarp sale say the format bears a strong resemblance to a slave market. "At first it seemed like you were going up like a bull for auction," said George Normand. "If you sell well, it's okay, but if you go for $7,000 you feel sick. It's embarrassing."

"The auction's not so bad," Buddy Bensmiller commented. "It doesn't take all that long."

The sale does have its bureaucratic inconsistencies. For a number of years, Wendel Eresman carried his own Eresman Brothers canvas at the Stampede. In order to run his own name, Eresman was placed in the bizarre situation of having to bid on himself. After purchasing his own canvas, he then had to pay ten to twenty percent of the bid price to the Calgary Stampede! Oldtimers Dick Cosgrave and Clem Gardner would have turned over in the grave to find they had to pay Calgary to carry their own names.

A number of potential sponsors also balk at having to pay 20 percent of their sponsorship money to the Calgary Stampede, but that format won't likely change. When the numbers were totalled in 1990, the Greatest Outdoor Show on Earth raked in almost twenty percent of the $1,120,500 bid on the drivers.

But many sponsors continue to bid every year and each has a different reason for getting involved.

Jim Bottomley of Majestic RV World is a longtime wagon sponsor who "Just loves the chucks." Ever since he was a boy growing up in Saskatchewan's ranching country, Bottomley had wanted either to drive or sponsor a chuckwagon. He does not discount the advertising value, but he is not sponsoring solely for company reasons.

Tom Glass and Totem Building Supplies make a dandy turn at Ponoka. At the 1991 and 1992 Canvas Auctions Totem secured a unique father-and-son racing team of Tom and Jason Glass.
(Targhee Photo by Gordon Biblow)

After noting the success of Calgary's program, Cheyenne Frontier Days initiated their own canvas auction. (The Wagner Perspective, photo by Randall A. Wagner)

Jim Thorogood of Totem Building Supplies loves the wagons as well, but also feels that sponsoring a wagon boosts his staff morale and helps to support Calgary's biggest drawing card, the Stampede.

After a good run with Hugh Sinclair in 1991, first-time sponsor Ted Valentine of Valentine Volvo said that he liked hearing Joe Carbury call his dealership's name over the loudspeaker to a packed grandstand.

In a Calgary Herald interview, PetroCanada spokesperson Judy Wish declared that their sponsorship of Kelly Sutherland was "money well spent," because employees all over Canada had a wagon to cheer for, and because PetroCanada wanted to be seen as a supporter of Calgary's Stampede.

Wayne Scaddan of the 1991 Stampede champion, Builders First, thoroughly enjoys the sport, and has become a member of the board of the WPCA. He appreciates the fact that there can be ". . . no phonies once the fellows get out there on the track." Scaddan was also impressed with the sense of co-operation in the chuckwagon business, and described watching veteran driver Dallas Dorchester take a rookie aside and show the young driver how to set his lead lines to keep them from catching in the wheelers' equipment.

But Scaddan also has an economic justification for sponsoring.

> In our first year of sponsorship we were only involved in the rural circuit (we were not in the Calgary Stampede). For an investment of $7,000 in sponsorship money we physically traced approximately $250,000 in sales directly attributable to the advertisement on chuckwagon tarps.

> The second year our sponsorship money increased to $32 000 and we competed in the Calgary Stampede. We had a record sales year, capturing 25% of the target market (Calgary construction lumber).

> Our third year, 1991, our sponsorship increased to $60,000 and we won the Calgary Stampede. The first five months of 1991were extremely slow . . . our entire country suffered from the economic slowdown [which] . . . lasted the entire year. However, our sales in the last six months [after the Stampede] are exactly double those of the first six months.

Scaddan also described how the company tracked its media exposure during the ten day Stampede and found that had they purchased the radio, television or media coverage it would have cost them almost one-half million dollars, not counting the presentation of the company name to the 18 000 people in the stands every night. The company felt that no other exposure could give those returns.

In some cases there is a camaraderie to sponsorship that suggests old-time loyalty to a roundup outfit. Supporters for the dual-sponsored Heritage Park/Calgary Co-op outfit speckle the grandstand with their distinctive yellow jackets. Other enthusiastic sponsors include the professionals who, over the years, collectively sponsored and signed the canvases of such outfits as "The Lawyers," "The Accountants," "The Partners," and "The Landmen."

Many sponsors take the time to learn about the sport, to become involved, and to become astute judges of men and horses. Those who paid the big prices at the 1991 Canvas Auction certainly knew what they were doing. The four finalists were the four top sellers:

PetroCanada's Kelly Sutherland, $79 000; Totem Building Supplies' Tom Glass, $67,500; Builders First's Dallas Dorchester, $60,000; and Majestic RV World's George Normand $57,000. Going into the last night's races, the four were bunched within one and two-hundredths of a second of one another, an amazing result after nine nights of racing, and an amazing feat for the sponsors who had selected the top four rigs.

Mosquito Creek wagon in a 1920s Calgary Stampede parade. Pioneer rancher Fred Ings is riding
directly behind the wagon.
(Glenbow Museum NA-466-38)

running by the rules

Four wagons, twenty men and thirty-two horses charging in tight circles and breaking out to thunder around a track only inches from each others' hooves and wheels, yet finishing one and two-hudredths of a second from one another. It is a thrilling experience for audiences in Calgary and around the world via television. It is an experience that wavers between thrill and terror for members of the wagon crews. The element that often makes the difference between those two emotions is the set of rules that govern the sport, and the skill and determination with which the rules are administered before, during and after a race.

The first few years of chuckwagon racing operated on a pretty haphazard basis. Interviews with old-timers describe unfortunate incidents that spurred the creation of new rules to keep those incidents from happening again. Ironically, a set of rules developed by the Boy Scouts for their winter ice stampede gave the wagon races their basic format.

A seated judge studies his time and penalty card. (Cosgrave Family Collection)

Rules are made by people, enforced by people, and followed by people, and this frequently makes for interesting situations.

Didsbury's Norm Haynes has been head judge for the Calgary Stampede chuckwagon races since 1965, but his involvement in the sport dates back much further.

Billy Haynes, Norm's father, outrode for the winning Sheep Creek outfits in 1934 and 1939. Norm grew up around the racetracks of southern Alberta and was jockeying at twelve. Former driver Bill Hamilton recalled that young Haynes was one of the most sought-after jockeys for Sunday afternoon match races. "The day after Calgary was over we had the track all to ourselves. Every wagon outfit had at least one or two good running horses and we'd race to see which were the fastest. Normie Haynes and Iris Glass were the jockeys everybody wanted to ride."

Norm Haynes checks the cinch on his mount.
(Haynes Family Collection)

Norm Haynes remembers riding against Iris, "lots." He graduated from jockeying to outriding in 1947, and in 1950 he and his father both outrode for Bob Heberling's winning outfit at Calgary. From 1951 to 1955, the younger Haynes joined Hank Willard's victorious crew on Calgary's grandstand stage four times. Norm followed Lloyd Nelson's winning rig in 1956, and the next year he mounted the stage again with Dale Flett's first championship outfit. His eight-year streak ended when Bill Greenwood won Calgary for Merle Anderson in 1958. That time the Haynes family was represented on the stage by Norm's brother George. From 1959 to 1962 Norm won three more championships with Dale Flett's Peter Bawden Rig.

If ever an all-star outriding team were declared, there is little doubt that Norm Haynes would be among the four. He had the respect of peers Lark IsBell and Bill Richardson and was considered the best by top drivers Dale Flett and Lloyd Nelson. Nelson also appreciated Haynes' gallant custom of acknowledging his driver before each race with a smile and a salute.

The last night of the 1963 Stampede Haynes was in line for another championship buckle when his outriding career came to an abrupt halt.

> I was riding a good derby horse named King's X. He'd been outrode two or three times each day during the week, and he'd been ridden in a consolation heat that morning. We were going down the backstretch and King's X was running along good, but he was on the right lead. Now if you want a horse to turn to the left, you want him on the left lead so I remember I shifted my weight to change his lead. King's X must have been tired, because his legs crossed and down he went.

The heavy pall of backstretch dust made it impossible for the other outriders to see; two more men went down as their horses stumbled over the fallen horse and rider. Haynes and another outrider were rushed to the hospital after the wreck.

Norm did not return to outriding. He wanted to keep some connection with the wagons, however, and when the opportunity arose, he became a chuckwagon judge at the Calgary Stampede. He'd been a hard-riding competitor on the track; he took the same code of conduct into the judging game. When he felt he was right, Haynes wasn't afraid to make a difficult or controversial call and take responsibility for it. This attitude quickly vaulted him into the position of head chuckwagon judge.

During the 1970s he encountered a number of difficulties with the system of appointing judges. "Until 1979, when the CRCA wagon men boycotted Calgary," Haynes said, "we paid out all the money, but they set their own rules . . . and brought their own judges. Back then a lot of the judges were friends of the wagon men; they hauled their horses and all. If I had a judge who made a good call – a driver came wide and the judge hit him with a stiff penalty – well, that judge wouldn't be back the next year. It takes two or three years to train a guy, so consequently we were picking up new judges every year."

Since the judges had been members of the breakaway CRCA, Haynes took the opportunity to hire new people and train them to call infractions consistently.

There are now eight judges, plus the chief, in the Eye In The Sky: two for each barrel. One watches the wagon and one the outriders. Most are experienced chuckwagon drivers and/or outriders. There is also a judge positioned at the clubhouse turn; one on the backstretch; and Haynes hired an ex-RCMP officer to handle breathalyzer checks.

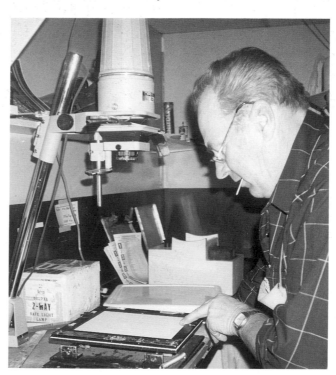

> It's only been since 1979 that I've had control over who's judging . . . Since 1979 none of my judges go near the barn. They don't even know a lot of the drivers, but they know every rule, they look at the films and they call every race the same.

The judges watch the drivers, the outriders, and sometimes more importantly, the horses. "When the fellow out in front starts cutting down to the rail," Haynes explained," and you see the inside driver throw his feet up on the front of the box and lean back like he's really pulling, you don't give inter-

Official race timer Bill Fraess studies the latest photo-finish print to determine the four wagons' exact times.
(Trudy Cowan, Museum of the Highwood)

ference penalties just for that . . . because what he could be trying to do is get you to think the other guy cut him off. What you've got to do is watch the horses' heads. If their heads stay right in there, you know they're not being pulled on. Those old drivers are smart and tricky; they're all playing games."

"Take false starts," he continued. "Back when I was riding for Lloyd Nelson and Hank Willard, one of the tricks was to have a false start, to break the rhythm of the other fellow's outfit. You knew that some horses just couldn't take those false starts, so one of the ploys

A sample photo finish print. The time of each wagon is determined by laying a straight edge from the lead horse's nose to the number chart below.
(Calgary Exhibition and Stampede)

was to pull out a couple times and get that fellow's horses so hot and bothered that they wouldn't work right. If a fellow pulls out now, we slap a penalty on him."

Haynes recalled that the Chuckwagon Rules Committee decided to change things to the way they thought chuckwagon racing should be run, and by the time the professional wagons returned to the Calgary track, the rules were established. "If they don't want to play by our rules," he said, "they don't come. They put up a $750 performance bond and sign a contract agreeing that we have the authority to keep the bond and send them home. If they break the rules to the extent they have to be replaced, we have a standby outfit ready. We needed one the year Kelly Sutherland went fishing over in Kelowna. Ed Alstott was there to replace him."

Every year, there is a meeting with the drivers the night before the races to go through the rule book together so there are no surprises. Sometimes a rule change is initiated during the week.

> For all the years I outrode, I saw guys come around the last corner and push the guy beside him to the outside so that one of his buddies could come through on the rail. It was wet right along the rail this one year, and some drivers were pushing the other guys out, guys who were in contention to win the show.

A special meeting was called immediately after that Thursday race and the rule was changed effective the next night. "Just like any other race," explained Haynes. "At the head of the stretch the leader must select his position, so the guys behind him can go to his right or his left. It gives them the opportunity to select their position. That's why we're having so many chuckwagons now finishing three or four abreast, lots of them."

In the late 1980s, an outrider lane was approved. This was a safe area fifteen feet wide along the outside, from the pole at the beginning of the homestretch to the finish line. A wagon can go in there, "but only so long as he doesn't bother the outriders." This is a far cry from the days when wagons had the right of way, and the outriders had to be constantly on guard.

A few drivers used to take a number of practice turns, or run a long way down the backstretch on a practice run, and the races were taking longer and longer to complete – hard on both the horses and the audience. "We changed the rules so they line up in reverse order when they come in and only take one practice turn . . . Now we can run the show off in fifty-five minutes," said Haynes.

Some of the old-timers feel that the spate of new regulations have spoiled the sport, but Haynes counters with statistics that show "we haven't killed a horse in three years."

"Our interference rule now is 'two plus.' If a wagon hub hits a wagon hub, it's steel on steel and a two second penalty; but if it is steel on flesh, on a horse, right now you get five, six, maybe ten seconds if the outfit can't come back to salute the grandstand after the race."

Every aspect of the race is examined. At one point the judges realized that the "bottom outfits" were getting no money at all, even though it cost them just as much to feed their horses and travel, so they changed the system for paying day money and now guarantee every outfit that qualifies to come to Calgary at least twenty-five hundred dollars, "even if they finish last every night."

The wagons themselves have come under a lot of scrutiny. In 1986, poor driver judgement combined with the low-slung design of the stove rack contributed to a spectacularly gruesome accident that saw men and horses flung like rag dolls across the racetrack. To ensure that such a disaster never occurred again, the offending driver was assessed a punishing thirty seconds in penalties, and the Calgary Stampede moved to change the stove rack. Norm Haynes was given the job of coming up with a better design.

"That gave my wife Gwen and me something to do. First we had to buy an old type of chuckwagon." When word got out that the Calgary Exhibition and Stampede was looking for a wagon, "The price started out quite low, but pretty soon these old beat-up chuckwagons that had been lying outside were getting kind of expensive." After some stiff negotiating, they bought one from Wendel Eresman, and the work of redesigning it began. "I had a young fellow working for me at Canadian Western Natural Gas," Haynes recalled.

When wagons are on the track at least one of the eight wagon and outrider judges must remain on duty in the eye-in-the-sky. Notice the four wagon judges' starting switches, and the master switch (far right, controlled by Norm Haynes). All five must be engaged before the starting klaxon will sound. (Trudy Cowan, Museum of the Highwood)

"He had taken a drafting course and I told him that we wanted to put this stove rack inside the wagon so that a horse's nose would hit the back of the wagon before its feet went in the rack."

Haynes had the carpenters tear the wagon down five times before he was satisfied, extending the wagon box to eleven foot four inches so that the stove rack fit completely inside. Drivers appreciated the new, safer design, with Ward Willard commenting, "How often have you stumbled over a coffee table? That's what the old stove rack was like for a horse."

Because the new enclosed stove rack was suspended high up out of the way, Haynes and his committee decided to change to a lighter, less cumbersome stove. He settled on a design developed by NPCA driver, Ray Croteau, consisting of two rubber feed buckets bolted together to make a cask shape. When left behind, this flexible "stove" has proven to be much safer than its predecessors which could become horse-crippling obstacles.

The two barrels around which every wagon turns a figure eight began as just that, wooden kegs with steel hoops, heavy enough to cause a wagon to tip, or leave dangerous splinters of wood or fragments of metal in the dirt when they got smashed.

Over the years barrels were changed to metal drums, then to heavy cardboard, finally to the current synthetic rubber tube which safely collapses when touched by wheel or hoof. As well as moving the stove rack into the wagon box, other changes have been made to the wagon itself, and the rules are strictly administered. Every year the wagons are weighed and inspected before they race at Calgary. This has provided a uniformity that is being felt in The Northern Professional, North Peace and World Professional Chuckwagon Association races.

For many years the exposed stoverack endangered the limbs and lives of outriding and chuckwagon horses. (Glenbow Museum NA-1241-900)

Haynes said, "We did a complete survey on every wagon: we checked every hub; we checked the poles, the reaches, measured all the hoops . . . some of them were running fairly light, some as much as a hundred and seventy pounds [77 kg] light. The old system was an honor system — it was up to each association to make sure their wagons weighed 1 325 pounds [602 kg] with the driver."

Because there was a great deal of controversy over the weights, the Stampede allowed drivers to protest if they thought another driver had an advantage because of an under-weight wagon. To discourage frivolous protests, the previous protest fee was raised.

"Right away who else but Kelly Sutherland sent over a cheque for a thousand dollars and two written protests to check Ray Croteau and Ray Mitsuing's wagons," Norm continued. "Croteau was okay, so Kelly lost $500, but Ray Mitsuing was 47 pounds [21 kg] light. He was fined one thousand dollars and just the night before Mitsuing had made $999 – the Stampede paid it out with one hand and took it back with the other."

Other non-regulation aspects of the wagons were found during inspections, such as three wagons with truss rods sticking a couple of inches out from the axle. Haynes asked what the rods were for, but nobody answered. "I knew it was to hook another guy's wagon wheel," he said seriously. "What else could it be for? So we made them get a hacksaw and saw them off."

It is virtually impossible for a horse to put its leg inside the modified stoverack. (Doug Nelson photo)

The crew consists of driver and four outriders. Going to and from the track the driver was allowed helpers. Haynes found that "it got so they had three or four people on board." When some drivers complained that they needed help to prevent runaways of the high strung animals, he countered with, "What the heck are you doing here if you can't hold your horses?"

But the judges realized that drivers did need help in some circumstances, so they ruled that the leaders must have halters on, and the Stampede brought in mounted riders to escort the wagons. Haynes added, "Having a mounted rider dressed in the Calgary Exhibition colors alongside an outfit looks good too, even if he doesn't do anything."

The mounted escort also makes sure that wagons do a complete salute to the grandstand at the end of their race. Winners are eager to show their sponsors' name to the full length of the stands, but, as Haynes explained, "the guys that lose or mess up, they sometimes want to turn around at the first barrel," and the Stampede felt that sponsorship deserved the exposure.

Wide gauge mountain wagon running gear, used under both the roundup and racing chuckwagons. Tom Glass and Richard Cosgrave had these axles and wheels shipped up from Kentucky.
(Doug Nelson, Museum of the Highwood)

Many things about chuckwagon racing have changed over the years, such as the configuration and length of the track, even the dirt itself. Today the dirt is a special composition of sand, chemically treated to minimize the dust that used to blind riders, particularly as the evening sun at race time slanted right into their eyes. Every rule, every change to equipment that is instituted helps to balance the skills and experience of the men and their horses with the chances that they take every night on the track. And the head judge at Calgary isn't through yet. "We're still in a process of changes that will make for better, safer wagon racing."

Just like any other vehicle, chuckwagons must be maintained
properly. Jerry Bremner greases his wagon.
(Doug Nelson, Museum of the Highwood)

Early Calgary Stampede judges perched in a booth with a great view of the finish line and infield.
(Cosgrave Family Collection)

Calgary's mounted riders do look good.
(Bob Morrison photo)

the next chapter

Two days after the start of the 1991 Calgary Stampede, on Saturday, July 6, the great veteran driver Tom Dorchester died.

The next evening after the final race, the outriders refrained from their normal routine of whooping down the track waving their hats to the crowd. Instead they formed a track-wide line and followed sixteen year old Tommy Quinn Dorchester in a solemn walk in front of the grandstand.

With driving lines tight, Tom and Joy Dorchester parade son Dallas' outfit in front of the Ponoka grandstand.
(Targhee Photo by Gordon Biblow)

Tuesday morning at 7:30 a.m., family and friends joined Tom Dorchester's son Dallas, to board a Greyhound bus at the Stampede Grounds. The Usona Hall overflowed with the 700 who gathered to say a final farewell. It was fitting that Joe Carbury, who had described so many of Tom's triumphs on the racetrack, should read his eulogy.

A group of sad faces arrived back at the grounds that afternoon. They knew that the Calgary Stampede would never be the same without the smiling face and the fun that Tommy D created.

Bill Kehler, who worked with Dorchester on CFAC radio's broadcast crew, remembered. "Tom Dorchester carried a paddle to stir the big pot. He kept everybody going with his tricks and jokes . . . he never would let anybody get the better of him on a joke."

Dorchester's old friend Orville Strandquist summed it up, "Tom was a good old boy, he always had fun. We're going to miss him."

Tom's friends and colleagues knew that the head of the Dorchester clan would not have wanted them to agonize over his passing. After doctors informed him of the cancer that had invaded his body, Tom told his wife Joy that he was prepared to die. "I've had a good, long life."

Only hours after the funeral, the wagons were rolling again in Calgary. Tom would have smiled at the results: Dallas had drawn the difficult number four barrel position, but spurred on by a desire to honor his father's memory, he lined his horses around the figure eight and fired onto the track first. As he shot past the grandstand stage, Dallas thought he saw his Dad standing in his regular spot on the stage with papers in his hand, waving him on and shouting, "Go on boy! Go on with it!" just like he had three years before when Dallas had almost won the $50,000 final.

Dallas took the day money with the fastest time of the night, and after five nights was ahead of Kelly Sutherland, and in the lead.

Dallas and Sutherland continued running neck and neck, and by Saturday night both drivers qualified for the winner-take-all final heat, the run for $50 000. Sutherland was first, winning the aggregate title with a time of 11:57.65; Dallas Dorchester second with 11:58.52; third – but still within one second of the leader – was George Normand, with 11:58.62; and the fourth finalist, Tom Glass, came in with 11:58.67.

All day Sunday the barns buzzed with excitement as 36 outfits prepared for the last race of the 1991 Calgary Stampede, but the majority of the speculation revolved around which of

Ray Mitsuing brushes dried mud off his lines.
(Trudy Cowan, Museum of the Highwood)

the top four might win the $50,000. Sitting in first, Sutherland was the odds-on favorite, but the sentimental favorite was Tom Dorchester's son Dallas. Everyone knew that George Normand's strong-finishing outfit would be close at the wire, and although few experts gave Tom Glass much of a chance of winning the race outright, they all knew that the winner would need a clean run, and Glass and his crew had run all week without penalties.

If all else remained equal, the outcome might rest on the barrel draw. Normally number one was the choice barrel position, but in 1991 the bronc chutes had been moved closer to the grandstand. As a result there was even less room than normal between the chutes and the top barrel, making number one a treacherous draw. That year the drivers' choice was number two.

Because the barrel draw for the final didn't occur until immediately after the sixth heat, the drivers had no chance to develop a hard and fast race strategy.

Back in 1987, Ray Croteau and Kirk Sutherland wait for Tom Glass to draw as
Kelly Sutherland studies his barrel position in the infield.
(Bob Morrison photo)

To maintain his position as aggregate leader, Sutherland had driven hard during the nine days, taking a toll on his stable. By the final day he had no choice as to which horses he would run Sunday evening. He only had four animals that he felt were fit enough to run for the $50,000, so only four wagon horses had their heads tied up in Kelly Sutherland's barn Sunday afternoon.

George Normand had brought two top turning and running outfits to Calgary. He selected the team that handled the Calgary track best and hoped for an inside barrel draw. Like Sutherland, Glass only tied up four wagon horses Sunday afternoon. But that knowledge did not stop him from being nervous. His wife, Joanne, related that he "stall-walked" all afternoon. Iris Glass added, "We just stayed away from Tom, stayed out of his way."

In his travels that afternoon, Tom Glass probably met Dallas Dorchester's sponsor, Wayne Scaddan, as he too wandered nervously through the barn alleys. But Scaddan was searching for his driver, and finally found Dallas and cohort Ken Bell in the Dorchester trailer, studying chuckwagon racing videos.

This was the fifth straight year Dallas would run in the final. He had come up short the previous four occasions and was not leaving anything to chance.

Unlike Sutherland and Glass, Dorchester had a selection of rested horses, so he and Bell were watching videos of the Dorchester outfits and their competitors to develop the best strategy for each barrel draw scenario: if he drew number one, he would hook his hardest starting and running outfit; if he were unlucky enough to draw number four, he would hook the strongest finishing team. For barrels two or three, they developed various combinations depending on which of their opponents drew the barrel position(s) inside their own. Bell wrote their options on four paper gunny sacks and nailed them to the tackroom wall.

Before the sixth heat and the barrel draw, they would have the four teams harnessed. Ken would stay at the barns. When he heard over the loudspeaker which barrel Dallas had drawn, and who was inside him, he would check the appropriate gunny sack and hook the designated team to their wagon.

Once the first race of the evening was underway, time passed quickly. It was not long before the sixth heat ended and the four $50,000 finalists piled into the back of the pickup that would take them from the chuckwagon barns over to the grandstand stage.

Just before they left, Dorchester told Bell to throw out all the options, to hook the slower turning and harder finishing outfit if he drew number four, and to hook the best starting and turning outfit if their draw was anything else but four. "You just can't win from behind," Dallas explained. "Not unless somebody else has problems. You have to hook your fastest start and turn." This sounded like advice from his father.

On the trip over to the grandstand, the four finalists visited amiably, but there was an undercurrent of nervous tension. They stepped out of the truck and mounted the stage.

As the aggregate winner, Sutherland had first draw. He reached into the box containing the barrel tokens, searched for a considerable time and pulled out – number one. He grinned and gave his thumb-up salute to the crowd. His action was greeted by applause sprinkled with a few boos. When Dallas stepped up, drew and displayed the number two, the crowd shared his pleasure. George Normand came next and picked number three, leaving Tom Glass the unenviable number four position.

The trip back to the barns was less tense. Pleased or disappointed, at least the suspense was over.

Before the men dispersed to prepare their outfits, they shook hands and wished one another luck, "Whether they meant it or not," Tom Glass noted later.

Glass' outfit had not been running as fast as the other three and he was very disappointed at his unlucky draw, but he was not giving up. "Anything can happen in a wagon race," he philosophized. The 1990 race was a prime example: Sutherland and Normand both hit barrels and Dorchester had an interference penalty, leaving Dave Lewis the $50,000 almost by default.

Ken Bell had the Dorchester horses hooked by the time Dallas returned. Dorchester stepped up onto the seat, took the lines and drove his outfit to the marshalling area at the southeast corner of the racetrack.

As the eighth heat competitors headed back to the barns, the boss of the marshalling area, Ralph Nelson, sent the four finalists toward the infield. They went in reverse order: Glass, Normand, Dorchester, and Sutherland. The men made their practice turns and reformed their original line, swung around and drove back to the infield. As the four wagons threaded their way into their barrel positions, the buzz of the crowd quietened to a hush.

Glass was in place, then Normand, then Dorchester. Sutherland's team pulled in last. They had barely stopped when the klaxon sounded.

Sutherland's horses hesitated a split second before jumping ahead and proceeding in a wobbly fashion toward the top barrel. In order to stay in the race Sutherland would have to cut the top barrel close, but he turned a fraction too soon. The barrel went down.

As the other three drivers made the top turn of their own figure eights, they each saw the fallen barrel. They knew it was now a three wagon race for $50,000.

The Dorchester wagon spun out onto the track first and sped to the first turn, but he was not far enough ahead to capture the rail from the tenacious Sutherland. As Dallas and Kelly raced side by side, George and Tom eased their rigs in behind. Around the second turn and down the backstretch, Dorchester's hard running team pulled away, but before he started into the third turn Dallas hauled back on his lines to slow his horses, giving them a moment to catch their breath. As the outfits swung around the last turn and lined out toward the homestretch, he let his horses resume their charge.

By that time, Normand's fast closing leaders were right behind Dallas' tailgate!

Normand couldn't believe Dorchester would take such a chance. After the race he enthused, "Only Dallas would have the balls to try a trick like that."

But the ploy worked. Having caught their second wind, the team proceeded to streak down the homestretch, crossing the line three-tenths of a second ahead of Normand. The Dorchester outriders, Jim Nevada, Jim Shield, Jerry Bremner, and young Tommy Quinn sitting atop his grandfather's outriding horse Ering, were all close behind their wagon.

Dallas drove his proudly prancing team back in front of the grandstand to receive the winner's applause. He stopped and stepped down. With his wife Shirley, their son Quinn and the other outriders, he climbed the steps onto the grandstand stage. Troy Dorchester gave his uncle Dallas a grey felt hat that had belonged to Tom Dorchester. Dallas replaced his battered straw hat with his father's stetson as he stepped forward to receive the 1991 Calgary Stampede chuckwagon championship awards.

During the race, announcer Bill Kehler had been in his regular spot on the grandstand stage, a spot he had shared with Tom Dorchester for almost ten years. As Dallas had spun off the barrels, Kehler was sure he heard a familiar voice shout, "Shake it at 'em boy!"

When Dallas reached for the grandstand microphone, there were tears in his eyes and his voice wavered, "This one's for you, Dad."

The days of the open range may be past, but the chuckwagon thunders into the future.
(The Calgary Herald Collection, Glenbow Museum)

appendix

of winners

Calgary Exhibition and Stampede winners since chuckwagon race inception in 1923:

Legend
+   All locations in Alberta unless otherwise denoted.
*   Dale Flett injured during show, replaced by Walgenbach.
** Dale Flett injured before show, replaced by Greenwood.
#   NCA & Independent competitors replace CPRA (WPCA) drivers.
Both NCA and WPCA drivers invited to compete.

Year	Driver	Outfit Sponsor(s)
1923	Bill Sommers, Nanton +	Cross, Drumheller, Macleay and Riley – Mosquito Creek pool wagon
1924	Tom Lauder, Huxley	Bagley and Lauder
1925	Jim Ross, Elnora	Collins and Ross
1926	Dick Cosgrave, Cheadle	Millars & Cosgrave
1927	Tom Lauder, Innisfail	Tom Lauder
1928	Tom Lauder, Innisfail	Tom Lauder
1929	Jim Ross, Elnora	Jim Ross
1930	Dick Cosgrave, Michichi	Dick Cosgrave
1931	Clem Gardner, Pirmez Creek	Clem Gardner
1932	Jim Ross, Elnora	Jim Ross
1933	Dick Cosgrave, Wayne	Dick Cosgrave
1934	Eben Bremner, Dewinton	Goettler & Hamilton – Sheep Creek pool wagon
1935	Dick Cosgrave, Rosebud	Dick Cosgrave
1936	Dick Cosgrave, Rosebud	Dick Cosgrave
1937	Dick Cosgrave, Rosebud	Dick Cosgrave
1938	Dick Cosgrave, Rosebud	Dick Cosgrave

Year	Driver	Outfit Sponsor(s)
1939	Sam Johnson, Dewinton	Goettler & Hamilton Sheep River Creek pool wagon
1940	Dick Cosgrave, Rosebud	Dick Cosgrave
1941	Ron Glass, Bowness	Lunseth & Higgins
1942	Dick Cosgrave, Rosebud	Dick Cosgrave
1943	Dick Cosgrave, Rosebud	Dick Cosgrave
1944	Theo Thage, Halkirk	Theo Thage
1950	Bob Heberling, Rosebud	Bob Heberling
1951	Hank Willard, Milo	Willard & Nelson
1952	Hank Willard, Milo	Commodore Allen
1953	Hank Willard, Milo	Commodore Allen
1954	Hank Willard, Milo	Commodore Allen
1955	Hank Willard, Milo	Hank Willard
1956	Lloyd Nelson, High River	L. O. Nelson
1957	Dale Flett, Handhills	Peter Bawden
1958	Bill Greenwood, Lousana	Merle Anderson
1959	Dale Flett/Hally Walgenbach*	Peter Bawden
1960	Hally Walgenbach, Stettler	Orville Burkinshaw
1961	Hally Walgenbach, Stettler (tie) Dale Flett, Handhills	Orville Burkinshaw Peter Bawden
1962	Dale Flett, Handhills	Peter Bawden
1963	Dale Flett, Handhills	Peter Bawden
1964	Hally Walgenbach, Stettler	Pratt & MacKay
1965	Bill Greenwood, Lousana	Janko Bros.
1966	Bill Greenwood, Lousana**	Sigurd Nielson
1967	Bob Cosgrave, Handhills	Flett Bros.
1968	Garry Dorchester, Westerose	Denham Bros.
1969	Bob Cosgrave, Handhills	John Irwin
1970	Tom Dorchester, Westerose	Jack Sheckter
1971	Tom Dorchester, Westerose	Stewart Ranches
1972	Ralph Vigen, Grande Prairie	R. J. Keen
1973	Slim Helmle, Esterhazy, Sask.	Merle Anderson
1974	Kelly Sutherland, Grande Prairie	Norman Nilson
1975	Kelly Sutherland, Grande Prairie	Norman Nilson
1976	Ralph Vigen, Grande Prairie	Northern Metallic
1977	Kelly Sutherland, Grande Prairie	Archie Hackwell
1978	Kelly Sutherland, Grande Prairie	Maclin Ford
1979	Buddy Bensmiller, Dewberry [#]	Lloydminster Spill

178

Year	Driver	Sponsor
1945	Alvin Hilker, Red Willow	Alvin Hilker
1946	Ron Glass, Torrington	Johnny Phelan
1947	Ron Glass, Torrington	Johnny Phelan
1948	John Swain, Innisfail	J.J. Swain
1949	Ron Glass, Torrington	Johnny Phelan

Year	Driver	Outfit Sponsor
1980	Herman Flad, Bodo	Commanche Drilling
1981	Bruce Craige, Dewberry	Century 21
1982	Dave Lewis, Grande Prairie ##	Panee Memorial Agriplex
1983	Tom Glass, High River	Gulf Canada
1984	Dallas Dorchester, Falun	J & L Supply Co. Ltd.
1985	Ralph Vigen, Grande Prairie	Goodstoney Rodeo Centre
1986	Kelly Sutherland, Grande Prairie	Cambridge Shopping Centres
1987	Tom Glass, High River	Calgary Herald
1988	Dave Lewis, Grande Prairie	White Spot
1989	Buddy Bensmiller, Dewberry	Chinook Centre
1990	Dave Lewis, Grande Prairie	Western Gas
1991	Dallas Dorchester, Falun	Builders First
1992	Tom Glass, High River	Totem Building Supplies

Cowboys Protective Association (CPA), Canadian Rodeo Cowboys Association (CRCA), Canadian Professional Rodeo Association (CPRA), and World Professional Chuckwagon Association (WPCA) circuit winners since initial chuckwagon accreditation in 1949:

> Legend
> + All locations in Alberta unless otherwise denoted.
> * Represents dollars won during that year.
> ** Point system instituted.

Year	Driver	Outfit Sponsor	Points
1949	Lloyd Nelson, High River +*	Willard & Nelson	1 809
1950	Ron Glass, Torrington	Johnny Phelan	1 696
1951	Ron Glass, Torrington	Johnny Phelan	2 014
1952	Ron Glass, Torrington	Johnny Phelan	4 186
1953	Hally Walgenbach, Stettler	Hally Walgenbach	4 882
1954	Hank Willard, Milo	Commodore Allen	3 451
1955	Hank Willard, Milo	Hank Willard	3 905
1956	Lloyd Nelson, High River	L. O. Nelson	3 933
1957	Dale Flett, Handhills	Peter Bawden	6 201
1958	Bill Greenwood, Lousana	Merle Anderson	6 328
1959	Dale Flett, Handhills	Peter Bawden	5 995
1960	Hally Walgenbach, Stettler	Orville Burkinshaw	5 052
1961	Dale Flett, Handhills	Peter Bawden	6 249
1962	Dale Flett, Handhills	Peter Bawden	4 474
1963	Ralph Vigen, Grande Prairie	Claggett Bros.	5 567
1964	Hally Walgenbach, Stettler	Pratt & MacKay	6 537

Year	Driver	Outfit Sponsor	Points
1965	Ron Glass, High River	Fiesta Farms	5 990
1966	Tom Dorchester, Westerose	Jack Sheckter	9 358
1967	Bill Greenwood, Lousana	Janko Bros.	8 716
1968	Garry Dorchester, Westerose	Denham Bros.	8 179
1969	Tom Dorchester, Westerose	Jack Sheckter	9 075
1970	Tom Dorchester, Westerose	Stewart Ranches	11 047
1971	Tom Dorchester, Westerose	Stewart Ranches	10 954
1972	Ralph Vigen, Grande Prairie	R. J. Keen	10 947
1973	Dave Lewis, Grande Prairie	Lyle Adams	9 188
1974	Kelly Sutherland, Grande Prairie	Norman Nilson	9 879
1975	Ralph Vigen, Grande Prairie	Northern Metallic	15 316
1976	Ralph Vigen, Grande Prairie	Northern Metallic	15 444
1977	Kelly Sutherland, Grande Prairie	Archie Hackwell	19 075
1978	Ralph Vigen, Grande Prairie	Rimrock Drilling	24 578
1979	Kelly Sutherland, Grande Prairie	Maclin Ford	27 612
1980	Tom Glass, Okotoks	Gulf Canada	22 727
1981	Tom Glass, High River **	Gulf Canada	481
1982	Kelly Sutherland, Grande Prairie	Maclin Ford	343.5
1983	Kelly Sutherland, Grande Prairie	Calgary Herald	302
1984	Dallas Dorchester, Falun	J & L Supply Co. Ltd.	346.5
1985	George Normand, Bonnyville	Den Mar Construction	249
1986	Mel Haase, Grand Centre	Haase Welding	213
1987	George Normand, Bonnyville	Majestic RV World	267
1988	Tom Glass, High River	Calgary Herald	334
1989	George Normand, Bonnyville	Majestic RV World	344.5
1990	Jerry Bremner, Westerose	Western Heritage Centre	357
1991	George Normand, Bonnyville	Majestic RV World	448
1992	George Normand, Bonnyville	Majestic RV World	504

Cheyenne Frontier Days Champions from chuckwagon race inception in 1952:

Legend
* Records incomplete; Gooch believed to be winner.
+ All locations in Alberta unless otherwise denoted.
# NCA & Independent competitors replace WPCA drivers.
** Records unclear; each name appears on a winner's list.

Year	Driver
1952	Buster Rusk, Missoula, Montana
1953	Jack Gill, Gadsby, Alberta
1954 *	Phil Gooch, Milo, Alberta
1955	Tom Dorchester, Westerose +
1956	Ron Glass, Torrington

Year	Driver
1957	Hally Walgenbach, Stettler
1958	Hally Walgenbach, Stettler
1959	Tom Dorchester, Westerose
1960	Ralph Vigen, Grande Prairie
1961	Dale Flett, Handhills
1962	Dale Flett, Handhills
1963	Bill Greenwood, Lousana
1964	Bob Cosgrave, Handhills
1965	Bob Cosgrave, Handhills
1966	Ron Glass, High River
1967	Bob Cosgrave, Handhills
1968	Bill Greenwood, Lousana
1969	Bob Cosgrave, Handhills
1970	Ron Glass, High River
1971	Kelly Sutherland, Grande Prairie
1972	Bill Greenwood, Lousana
1973	Ralph Buzzard, Chilliwack, British Columbia
1974	Tom Glass, High River
1975	Orville Strandquist, Stettler
1976	Tom Glass, Okotoks
1977	Ward Willard, Vulcan
1978	Ward Willard, Vulcan
1979	Ward Willard, Vulcan
1980	Kelly Sutherland, Grande Prairie
1981 [#]	Herman Flad, Bodo
1982	Buddy Bensmiller, Dewberry
1983	Buddy Bensmiller, Dewberry
1984	Buddy Bensmiller, Dewberry
1985 [**]	Herman Flad, Bodo or Ray Croteau, Bonnyville
1986	Ray Croteau, Bonnyville
1987	Buddy Bensmiller, Dewberry
1988	Ray Mitsuing, Loon Lake, Saskkatchewan
1989	Buddy Bensmiller, Dewberry
1990	Ray Mitsuing, Loon Lake, Saskatchewan
1991	Buddy Bensmiller, Dewberry
1992	Buddy Bensmiller, Dewberry

Northern Chuckwagon Association (NCA) since 1976:

Year	Driver
1976	Mel Haase, Grand Centre
1977-79	Allan Bensmiller, Dewberry
1980	Herman Flad, Bodo
1981	Leonard Ross, Meadow Lake, Sask.
1982	Allan Bensmiller, Dewberry
1983-87	Buddy Bensmiller, Dewberry

The NCA became the Northern Professional Chuckwagon Association (NPCA) in 1988. The winners since 1988 are:

Year	Driver
1988	Buddy Bensmiller, Dewberry
1989-90	Ray Mitsuing, Loon Lake, Sask.
1991-92	Buddy Bensmiller, Dewberry

glossary

of chuckwagon racing terms

The Horses:

Leader   –   member of the forward pair of a four horse outfit.

Team
  (outfit)   –   a horse hitch of two or more (normally four on a chuckwagon).

Wheeler   –   member of the rear pair of a four horse outfit (nearest the wagon).

The Human Competitors:

Driver   –   the person who sits on the wagon's seat and directs the horses.

Outrider   –   one of either two or four people who perform specific tasks during a race, including following their wagon to the finish line on horseback.

The Harness & Tack:

Bridle   –   straps for the horse's head which secure a bit in the animal's mouth; used in conjunction with driving lines or riding reins.

Blinkers   –   leather shields which flare off a horse's bridle next to its eyes and ensure the animal is not distracted by events immediately behind and beside it.

Halter: –   straps for the horse's head; used with a rope shank to control the animal as it is being held or led.

Hames   –   two J-shaped metal or wooden forms containing rivetted rings to which the tugs (traces) and the rest of the harness are attached. The two hames buckle together (by short straps) at the top and bottom to snugly fit a horse's collar.

Horse collar –   a thick oval form (usually made of leather and filled with horse-hair or straw) which fits over the withers and lower part of a horse's neck. A front facing rim supports the hames. Sometimes used in conjunction with felt or fabric cushions called sweat pads.

Lines	–	long leather straps held by a driver to control his team(s); attached to the horses' bridles with branching leather straps called crosschecks.
Reins	–	leather straps attached to a bridle's bit and used for control by a mounted rider.
Tugs (traces)	–	thick leather or nylon straps (often with chain link ends) which connect the hames to a doubletree (via the singletree) and allow the horse to pull a load.

The Wagon:

Canvas *(tarp)*	–	the cloth or plastic fabric which covers and protects the rear box section of a chuckwagon. In racing, it displays the name of the wagon's sponsor and its driver.
Doubletree	–	an approximately one metre (three foot) piece of hardwood or metal which bolts to the wagon pole (tongue) and to which the two singletrees are attached – can be lead or wheel doubletrees.
Neckyoke	–	a short, thick wooden or metal rod with a large "O"ring on either end: connected to the forward edge of the wagon pole. When secured with straps to the wheel horses' hames the neckyolk holds the pole off the ground.
Singletree	–	a short piece of hardwood or metal with a hook or ring at either end to which a tug may be attached. Connected by a ring or bolt to a double-tree.
Stove	–	originally a working metal stove weighing up to 32 kg (70 pounds). Later replaced by metal, cardboard or rubberized imitations. Loaded in a stoverack by an outrider at the beginning of a race.
Stoverack	–	a wooden or metal basket attached on the inside of a chuckwagon to carry either a real or simulated stove.
Tent pegs	–	two slim wooden or metal rods with weighted tips; used to support the chuckwagons rear tent flap – both flap and pegs are 1.6 metres (five feet six inches) long and are loaded by outriders into the wagon box at the beginning of a race.
Truss rods	–	a short rod projecting out from the centre of a wagon wheel's hub.
Wagon pole *(tongue)*	–	one long wooden or metal shaft connected to the front axle of a wagon – to which the doubletrees and neck yolk are attached.

The Racetrack and Infield:

Backstretch	–	the straightaway area farthest from the infield and grandstand.
Barrel	–	a wooden, metal, cardboard or rubberized cylinder, used in pairs as obstacles, around which each driver must make a figure eight turn at the start of a race.
Homestretch	–	the straightaway area of a racetrack which leads to the finish line in front of the grandstand.
Infield	–	the half-moon shaped enclosure directly in front of the grandstand which often encloses rodeo events as well as the barrel-turning setup for chuckwagon racing.
Klaxon	–	the loud horn which denotes the start of a race.
Long Barrel		the inside starting position with the farthest distance between the barrels.
Racetrack	–	an oval circuit around which horses run.

Miscellaneous Terms:

Coldblood	–	a horse with a background that includes other than thoroughbred breeding.
Cold-jaw	–	when a recalcitrant horse clamps the bit in his mouth so that the rider loses all control.
Heat	–	designation for a separate individual race on a racemeet program.
Hooked tough	–	denotes a driver placed in a heat with extremely challenging competition.
Penalties	–	extra seconds added to the running time of an outfit whose wagon or outriders violated race rules.
Stove up		for horses or men, freedom of movement impaired by either injury, age or disease.
Thoroughbred	–	a properly bred and registered racehorse, able to compete on recognized "A" and "B" circuit racetracks.

Organizations:

CPA	–	Cowboys Protective Association; initial professional Canadian rodeo cowboys' organization. Established in 1947.
CRCA	–	Canadian Rodeo Cowboys Association; an interim title for professional Canadian rodeo cowboys and associations.

CPRA	–	Canadian Professional Rodeo Association; present title of professional Canadian rodeo cowboys and associations.
NCA	–	Northern Chuckwagon Association; initial title used by chuckwagon drivers located in northeastern Alberta and northern Saskatchewan and Manitoba. Believed to have been established in 1976.
NPCA	–	Northern Professional Chuckwagon Association; version of the NCA (changed 1988).
WPCA	–	World Professional Chuckwagon Association; title assumed by the CPRA chuckwagon drivers after they separated from that organization in 1981.

A Few Range Wagon terms:

Grub (chuck)	–	food.
Remuda	–	herd of extra horses for trail drive and roundup.
Bed wagon	–	an extra wagon used on larger drives and many roundups which carried bedrolls, war bags, ropes and other bulky supplies.
Bedroll	–	various types of sleeping bags, usually consisting of wool blankets, or soogans, on the inside and a canvas groundsheet outside; sometimes shared by two cowboys.

sources

The Alberta Report.

The Albertan.

Bar U Ranch, National Historic Site, WRO, Calgary, 1992.

Breen, David H. *The Canadian Prairie West. The Ranching Frontier, 1874 - 1924.* Toronto: University of Toronto Press, 1983.

The Calgary Herald.

The Calgary Sun.

Crisman, Harry E. *America West.* [Athens, Ohio]: Swallow Press, n.d.

Godsal, F.W. Paper delivered to the Calgary Historical Society in the 1920s. Glenbow Archives.

Graber, Stan. "Matador Roundup and Trail Drive of 1921," *Grainews*, Winnipeg, Manitoba, 1991-1992.

The High River Pioneers' and Old Timers' Association. "Leaves from the Medicine Tree." *Lethbridge Herald,* 1960.

Hine, Robert V. *The American West.* Boston: Little, Brown & Co., 1973.

Kelly, L.V. *The Range Men.* Toronto: W.Briggs, 1913.

Ings, Fredrick William. *Before the Fences.* Calgary: McAra Printing, 1980.

Kennedy, Fred. *The Calgary Stampede Story.* Calgary: T. Edwards Thonger, 1952.

MacEwan, Grant. *Blazing the Old Cattle Trail.* Saskatoon: Western Producer Prairie Books, 1975.

MacEwan, Grant. *Wildhorse Jack.* Saskatoon: Western Producer Prairie Books, 1983.

McKinnon, C.H. *Events of LK Ranch.* Calgary: Phoenix Press, 1979.

McKinnon, Lachlin. *Lachlin McKinnon, Pioneer.* Calgary: McAra Printing, 1950.

Milo and District Historical Society. *Snake Valley.* Calgary: Friesen Printing, 1973.

Princess Patricia's Canadian Light Infantry. *RIC-A-DAM-DOO,* July 21, 1978.

Renno, Edward L. "The Wild and Wonderful Magic of the 101 Ranch," *Persimmon Hill,* 12, 3, [National Cowboy Hall of Fame and Western Heritage Centre, Oklahoma City] (1982).

Scaddan, Wayne. Letter to WPCA President Wayne Overacker. November, 1991.

Through the Years. Lousana Local History Society. Calgary: Friesen Printing, 1980.

Weadick, Guy, and Calgary Stampede Promotion.

index